Chariot of Fire

Elijah of the Last Days

The author's statement of faith:

Jesus Christ, the only begotten Son of God,
came in the flesh, shed His Holy Blood on
the Cross at Calvary for the sins of the world.
He is Lord of the universe, King of Kings

and I am His.

Martha Kilpatrick

ISBN 0-9665929-1-3

Artwork by
Bracha Brym-Lavee
M & B Studio, Jerusalem Israel

Cover Design and Graphics by
Vassiana Gargallo
Alexandria, Virginia

Shulamite Publishing
P.O. Box 30
Suches, GA 30572
866.311.4646
www.shulamitepublishing.com

Table of Contents

Introduction

There is the history of politics and
  there is the recorded story of nations.

But the authentic history is the unwritten record of
humanity, of people and their private stories,
  formed and composed by God and posted
  only in His Eternal Annals.

There are films of wars and documents of conflict.
  But the real war is fought individual by individual,
  a spiritual clash of heaven and hell
  fought in the solitary heart,
  and there in the secret recesses ..
  won or lost.

This is not a book I wanted to write.
It is a book I *had* to write.
And in the end, it has become a joy to offer it
to the Body of Christ, to those who bear the
anointing of Elijah
and recognize the torture of Jezebel.

I consider it my document of spiritual war,
a manual of enemy strategy,
but above all, an explosive declaration of Victory.

The Bible is about God… and man…
but something else as well.

The Bible's shocking content is very much about *evil*…
in all its deceiving faces and
its boring repetition.

We would rather turn our religious heads and
hope it goes away, this *evil*.
It doesn't.
For the ardent believer — seeking God's face —
this presence, this black opposition,
is around every corner.
It must be faced…
or it will consume your soul.

The assignment of God,
     the test of obedience,
          the crucible of purity…
is hidden inside how you deal with evil,
     with His rabid enemy.
It is a fearsome responsibility.
We would rather work than fight,
     dance than grapple.

But to fail to climb into your ring of conflict
     is to lose your chance at Divine Adventure,
          not to mention your Eternal Destiny.

Then Satan will write the final chapter of *your* story.

If you fail to face evil, and refuse to name evil,
     you *become* evil,
          and disastrously blind to it.
William Blake,
the great Christian poet of the 18th century wrote:

     "Bring me my bow of burning gold.
     Bring me my arrows of desire.
     Bring me my spear, O clouds unfold.
     Bring me my ***chariot of fire.***"

The fire of Elijah, blazing against satanic evil
is a missing quality in Christian men and women –
     therefore in the church.
The Chariot of fire must be restored to this generation,
     which could be the last one.

So…
to the **courageous,**
to the **desperate,**
come with me!
This seasoned and very scarred warrior
has some Light for your uphill path…
and some Very Good News.

**How I praise you, O my Father, for your Perfect Gift of
victory in the Only Begotten Son, Jesus Christ. Let that
Mighty Victory ring forth from these words and give
hope and triumph to your people.**
Even above that, Lord, *in* this writing
<u>may</u> <u>God</u> <u>be</u> <u>magnified</u>
and *by* this writing, satisfied.

Amen and amen!

Martha Kilpatrick

*"This is the judgment
that the Light has come into the world,
and men loved the darkness rather than the Light,
for their deeds were evil.
For everyone who does evil hates the Light,
and does not come to the Light for fear that
his deeds will be exposed."*
John 3:19,20

Tishbite in Israel

An unknown man,
an unknown past…
known to God.

Elijah Arrives

Elijah was a Tishbite.
Living remote from civilization,
he hid an entire history with God,
a story never disclosed.
It was preparation for his specific assignment from God.

His name means "Yahweh is God." Not Jezebel, not Baal...
God is God and Elijah was sent to prove it.

Out of that obscure past he stepped onto the stage of Israel's
apostasy as the pivotal figure in the drama of Jezebel and Ahab.
His mission from God: defeat them.
And solely on Elijah does the story turn.

The story holds an eternal secret; one that carries to the end of
the Bible's saga in Revelation 2. Not merely a Bible story of an
ancient past, it is a lesson for the Latter Days,
"before the great and terrible day of the Lord."
Malachi 4:5
At the end of the Old Testament is Elijah.
The promise of his return –
an Elijah-type of God's visitation –
is the significant close of the Old Testament.
Its final words...

"Behold I will send you Elijah the prophet,
before the coming of the great and dreadful
day of the Lord."
Malachi 4:5

**The nature of Elijah and the mission of Elijah
will return as God's provision
at the end of the age.**

The story holds the elements of the defeat of Jezebel and Ahab,
and the glorious rapture of Elijah.
So the primary enemy of the last days will be Jezebel,
and her defeat will be the prelude to the rapture.

So we watch for the revealing of the Elijah-visitation,
the effect of which will be to

*"turn the heart of the fathers to their children
and the hearts of the children to their fathers, or else
I will come and strike the land with a curse."*
Malachi 4:6

Elijah holds an exalted place in the
whole story of God's redemption.

He is honored as the supreme example of
answered prayer in James 5:16-18.

*"The earnest (heartfelt, continued) prayer of a righteous
man makes tremendous power available
(dynamic in its working)."*
Amplified Bible

Elijah, portrayed as fully human, was a commander
of heaven. Divine example of prayer.

"Elijah was a man with a nature like ours, and he
prayed earnestly that it would not rain; and it did not
rain on the land for three years and six months."

Elijah, the man **behind** the prayer…
   The words of prayer, the ideas of prayer, do not
      an answer make.
   The **life** of the one who prays
      determines the power of the answer.
   Elijah, filled with Divine Energy, and
        privy to the secret plans of God
        because of radical surrender…
      these are the means to answered prayer.

      Not how long you pray, not what you say,
      but **who** you are before His face… in secret.

By prayer Elijah ruled over the rulers
      of Israel: Jezebel and Ahab.
By prayer he brought in the dominion of God.
   "God is God!"
And that is what Elijah accomplished, demonstrated, proved.
      Oh, how wonderful!

      His life, the ultimate example of prayer
      that blasts heaven into earth!

Drought brings a people to their knees. It stands for the with-
drawing of God's blessing, the barrenness of
God's displeasure.
      It is meant to produce thirst –
      a thirst that turns to God for quenching.

Elijah was willing to commit his own existence to suffering
in order for the people to repent and turn back to God.

His goal was the defeat of Satan
who had destroyed the worship of God
through Jezebel and Ahab.
So his prayers were in harmony with heaven's
will and reign.

Elijah's life was lived in the mountain with God.
The mountain, a secret life higher than any other,
where that one lives in the presence of God
so intimately and for such long periods that
he/she knows the thoughts of God and
brings them down to earth in visible form.

"thy will be done on earth as it is in heaven."

In the Last Days, Elijah-prayer will return. God will in secret
mold the lives of many individuals until they possess His righ-
teousness. He will endue them with zeal for prayer and the
knowledge of His will.

They will hate evil without fear and attack it on their knees.
They will confront those in evil with a fierce likeness to Jesus,
with confidence and aggression.
They will rule nations – shake the kingdom of hell – and bring
God's reign into earth's final heavings.

People! Rejoice! Elijah is here!

Elijah's Mission

It seems that the primary goal, the central purpose for Elijah's
whole life, was the defeat of Jezebel. And when
        it was accomplished in promise
        (though Jezebel was not actually dead)
        Elijah went up in a "rapture."

In the end time the *type of person* God anoints
        to be like Elijah,
                will be assigned the defeat of Jezebel
                in preparation of the church for the rapture.

"Elijah" stands for an anointing of God,
                for an aspect of His nature He imparts
                        to the person chosen for this assignment.

        God's presence with John the Baptist bore a likeness
                to Elijah because it was the same manifestation of God.
                John's dress, his dwelling in the wilderness,
                his fire and boldness… these were like Elijah.
                And Jesus called him Elijah.

God, hating Jezebel, sends His Spirit of fierceness and war
        along with powerful authority to rest on those
                assigned to defeat the Jezebel-type.

        John's battle with Herodias was a fight with
        the evil presence of Jezebel in the woman
                who seduced her brother-in-law
        because he was king and she would be queen.

When Christ was born into the world,
Jezebel was sent by hell's master to
thwart His mission.
Jezebel is the most evil deception the
enemy uses against the 'Church' – the true believers.

Jezebel appears in force and power again
in the Last Days
because He is coming!
It's time again for Elijah and John the Baptist to
step on the scene for the battle with
Satan's scheme called Jezebel.

When the return of Christ is imminent, God sends the
anointing of Elijah to bring
the defeat of Jezebel in preparation of the Church
for the Second Coming of the Lord Jesus.

Believers must be set free of this satanic dominion,
and "Elijah" is sent for that purpose.

Jezebel is a principality
with a higher authority than a mere demon.
It is a power of the air. [1]

Jezebel stands for the hidden presence of Satan
behind a religious and powerful person.

[1] Ephesians 6:12

Behind such a human being is
a demonic power that will dominate any person
who invites this evil...
even a Christian.

Jezebel seeks a place inside the church.
The warning of Revelation 2:20 is to the believer,
not the unsaved.
The person who yields to the ways of Jezebel
(by the character flaw of self-promoting)
invites the presence of that hunting evil.

The proof of her presence:
religion,
women ruling and not serving,
weakness of men,
rampant sexual immorality,
homosexuality,
pornography,
incest,
impotence,
and a powerless Church.

Jezebel is here.

The Brook Cherith

You can't fight the Ancient Foe
until you know your Ruler rules

Ravens and Sovereignty
1 Kings 17

Evil reigned in Israel and the terror of that regime
   cannot be imagined.
Prophets were being slaughtered – every one.
Only those hidden by lawbreakers could survive
   the sword of Jezebel's zeal for her idol.
Blood flowed and no one was immune to its shedding.
   Not even Ahab's servants.

1 Kings 18:13

God arranged the safe hiding place of
   Elijah by the Brook Cherith.

    "Leave here… hide in the Kerith Ravine…"
verse 2

There, in marvelous symbol,
   the Father of Israel began to train the man.

Before you can glare into the face of tyranny,
before you can defeat Satan by fearless confrontation,
   you have to know who God is…
   and just how much He IS *God.*

The first knowledge about this All-Knowing Father is that
   He *will* take care of practical need.
   He knows we are frightened children made of dust.

Nothing was left without His tender provision
for a trembling servant.

*"You will drink from the brook, and
I have ordered the ravens to feed you there."*
verse 4

When you serve God, He sees **you are served** by
complete provision in the face of
the starvation of all others around you.

Water, symbol of the Spirit, the most
basic, fundamental,
spiritual, and physical need of humanity.

Water from a brook... the constant flow of the Spirit of God,
entering and refreshing you.

*"The ravens brought him bread and meat
in the morning and bread and meat in the evening"*
verse 6

Bread speaks of the presence of God as the
primary staff of life... basic existence.
Meat is the symbol for the strong truths of God,
only digestible to the mature...

Over and over,
meditating on the truths that seem least believable,
Elijah was sent to quiet seclusion, in order to "chew"
    on a startling revelation of God:
    He commands the ravens to His service!
    "I have ordered the ravens to feed you there."
        verse 4

Ravens are a Biblical symbol of evil.
They are scavengers, named unclean, and holy Israel
was forbidden to eat ALL types of them.   Deut.14:14

Yet the ravens were here used by God to
    sustain the very life of His choice servant!

When evil is rolling like a tide over a whole land,
evil seems to have mastered... even God.

Here, in a life hidden away, God was feeding Elijah with
    the Holy Spirit of His presence.
And the meat was the strong truth
    of **God's absolute sovereignty.**
Elijah would have to digest that Reality
    as food to dispel his fear.

Elijah had to learn
God could conquer the raven-evil by His overruling command.
He would transform even corruption into
   a life-sustaining miracle for Elijah.

Such a God few know.
To wrestle against evil and believe in its lying power
   is ignorance that God rules ravens.
      They are even His messengers…
        servants in the final end to His overriding purpose.

Few are the prophets who know such a Sovereign Lord.
   Undefeated Ruler over the universe, thwarted by none.

To be an Elijah requires just such a revelation of God
   as he met by the beak of a filthy, black raven.

Enemy Territory

The walls of evil
begin to crumble
by dislodging only one small brick.

Men and Fathers

In the end time, the type of person God anoints to be like
Elijah will be assigned the defeat of Jezebel in preparation of
the church for the rapture. The result will be that the fathers
will again have
> a heart for their children.

Jezebel turns men into Ahabs...
> weak, submissive men under her control.
> Men lose their fight, their emotional fire
> > and fierce virility.
> Laziness and excessive sleep steal in.
> A passivity without energy or zeal takes over in
> a man who is caught by the control of Jezebel.

She also made men eunuchs,
> who were then unable to have children at all.

When Jezebel, as a principality of Satan, is defeated, the
masculinity of men will be restored, and they will no longer be
captive and weakened by the enemy of their gender. Men will
be released both to bear (spiritual and natural) children and
to have a heart for them.

> Jezebel has been called the wife of Satan.
> As such, she attacks
> > the Bride of Christ.

Jezebel is confusion of gender.
> She was a queen who usurped the role as king.

Jezebel makes women masculine and men feminine.
> The homosexuality that is rampant is not
> merely a psychological problem,
> nor only about sin.

It is evidence of Jezebel's ruling,
> and those problems are hard to dislodge
> until the "strong man" is named… Jezebel.

Jezebel's special hatred is for maleness.
> The masculinity of Jesus is expressed
> in the prophetic office.

This manifestation of Jesus, the Great Prophet,
> was exhibited in Elijah.

The fierceness of Jesus and the exacting standard of God
> which was His zeal – this is the power of masculinity
> she seeks to neutralize so
>> the vitality of God in His Church is crushed
>> into insipid weakness.

The Elijah spirit of prophecy can dwell in a courageous woman
> as well as a man, just as the Jezebel spirit can
> operate through a man as well as a woman.

It is the *capacity for fierceness*
> in a prophetic person that speaks of the Elijah spirit.

This boldness was in John the Baptist as
> he confronted the Pharisees who inspected him,
>> and even in Herod, the king.

This characteristic of the fiery presence of God was in
Jesus when He turned over the
tables of the money changers in the temple.

It is the hatred of evil and the willingness
to assault it in the most courageous manner.
A boldness missing in so many leaders today –
leaders who will not fight or confront
and who excuse that cowardice as "Christian" kindness.

This boldness, this daring spirit, (in both – men and women)
Jezebel wants to destroy.

The Jezebel spirit cannot be overturned
without a ferociousness greater than her own.

The posturing of Jezebel is pictured in her great boasts
of dire consequences to Elijah.
Satan is always threatening as a means of
making a person submit through fear,
and by that fear… give up the fight.

Fear is the weapon of Jezebel and comes
by her threat of death.
The threat is not an idle one, as Jezebel arranged the
murder of all the prophets of God she could find.

Obadiah hid 100 prophets of God in caves and fed them there.
It is said of Obadiah that he "feared the Lord greatly."

Obadiah was caught between two fears:
   one fear of Jezebel and another of God.
   It takes great fear of God to go against
     Satan's terror-through-Jezebel.
Only such a fear of God will bring the obedience and courage
   it takes to defeat this evil.

Fear is what destroys masculinity and
   makes a man cower to the loss of
   his drive and dominion which is
     the fighting nature of his gender.

Fear is what causes a woman,
     in her feminine vulnerability, to operate in
     the control that invites the Jezebel spirit.

Jezebel invokes a fear that is beyond
       normal human dismay in life.
The fear Satan sends through Jezebel is debilitating.

What Elijah experienced under the juniper tree
   was not normal fear as all humans know it.
It was not a sudden cowardice that came out in the man.
   He had just won a great victory by the miracle of an
      unstarted fire.

   His fear was irrational, an assault of evil powers;
   a torturing terror of hell.

Suicidal despair and hopelessness are
    the experience of satanic fears.

People controlled by the Jezebel spirit through their sin,
    are those who harbor great rage and bitterness
with the delusion that their anger is
    justified and legitimate.

Satan rides this wrath and fans its flame with
    whispers of revenge and rights,
        then uses the fire to terrorize.

Unforgiveness is the root that grows a Jezebel.
    And intimidating anger,
        the fruit of her bitterness.

Fear is the trap that will silence and control people.
And fear is the response to Jezebel that makes for an Ahab.

The Widow and the Boy

God trains his conquerors in small battles
    with token victories that hold all the
    elements of the larger war.

David fought the lion and the bear to get ready
    for a mere Goliath.

Moses watched a dim-witted herd of sheep for 40 years
    and there he learned unending patience
    with wandering animals.
    Then! Then he was ready to lead five million,
    having been schooled on a few.

God will stretch you but never leaves you
    without a precedent...
    He has entirely too much integrity to
    assign a job about which you know nothing.

Elijah was commissioned to defeat Jezebel and
    he was sent in training to one widow and her son.
    When you confront the sin of a nation
    you do so beginning with only one.
    In that one... or two... you have the prototype
    to reveal the whole picture... and the solution.

And when you break the bondage of one, you have
    started to topple the walls of evil and
    the crumbling of its power has begun.

Elijah was to learn there in Zarephath the ways of his enemy,
the sinful issues that make Jezebel ruler of a life.
And the death-to-self it takes to come out.

Zarephath was a city in the region of Sidon, the place where
Jezebel's father was king It was her home, and the worship
center of her heathen god, Baal.

Elijah infiltrated that fortress built against the Most High God
to shake that spurious empire... from *within*.

Elijah would rescue two poor and obscure victims:
the widow and the boy.
To truly conquer evil, the one with an Elijah-bearing
enters the very life of the victim and by that
inside view conquers "the tyrant, Jezebel."

Such is the worth of an imprisoned-*one*
to the heart of God
that He would send His Choice Prophet
right into the village of the enemy.
There to live, serve and fight
until liberty was secured.

Elijah conquered the *domination of the widow*
and the *death of the boy*.
The roots of the Jezebel spirit.
The sins of men and the sins of women
displayed here in one small home.

The widow represents woman-without-man.
Jezebel's goal is the destruction of the male.
God is male. The Savior is male.
Masculinity came first in creation. Masculinity leads.
Femininity is not negated, God has His gentle character.
But without maleness and femaleness both, there is no life.

Jezebel, as Satan's disguise, wants the end of male firmness
so as to bring in a maelstrom; the utter confusion
in which the Enemy can take over.
So in Sidon the males were *gone.*
The woman-without-man is destitute. Fruitless and starving.
So also is the man-without-his-manhood.
The widow gripped her last bit of food,
a little flour, a cruse of oil.
And the prophet asked for it as a gift.

The woman in Jezebel is tempted to "own" in order to control.
Elijah touched the heart of the Jezebel ambition.
And the widow yielded.
The prophet brought the choice – from God – and it was
life or death.
Give up and live… or hold on and die.

Giving up control – that is the challenge of God.
To own is to lose His provision.
To relinquish – with all its terrifying risk –
is to feast during the famine of those who clutch.

Jezebel is the spirit of theft and murder, which is the essence of
   Satan's nature, brought to earth through a human-vessel
   who will share his ambition to possess.
Jezebel possessed her husband's position, the vineyard of
   Naboth, the prophets of God and all she owned
   she killed. This is the spirit of Jezebel.

The widow under the dominion of the Baal worship of her
country was tempted to solve life by the possessiveness of
Jezebel.
   Elijah showed her there was a choice,
      a different way.
   What a woman relinquishes to God is given
      back to her multiplied.
   A woman's strength lies in her feminine vulnerability,
      which God delights to cover.

Women without men can make miniature husbands of their
   sons, stripping them of golden fire
      and making them slaves of womanly fears...
   Such "boys" never escape the internal prisons
   that overbearing mothers have put them in
      and they perish there... little by little.

Wives can make little boys of their husbands,
   by taking the role of "mother" instead of "wife."

   The widow's boy began to die.

The NIV reads,
>*"the boy became ill and grew worse and worse."*

Women afraid, disappointed in men,
    often possess their sons and so take them over that
    their growth into manhood is stopped
        while they are yet boys
            their basic nature of fight and spit, violated…
            This is the Ahab spirit,
          the weakening of men unto the death
          of their very maleness.

Ahab-boys under Jezebel-widows die a slow and
    suffocating death.
          The death of individuality
          and therefore of energy
        and worse, the death of their gender,
          the male savagery
          God created and society needs.

When Jezebel rules, she kills maleness…
    Her ambition is not to be queen but to be king,
    with the privilege and power belonging to men.
    Her rival is not other women but other man.
When a woman assumes fierce dominance she is welcoming
    Jezebel evil.

Your spirit is your spirit but your soul has gender.
    The mind, will and emotions function
        according to gender.

Marriage will not exist in heaven, neither will pastors,
  prophets, family relationships...
  but gender remains forever.

When the woman gives into fear and greed,
  she invites the Jezebel ways.
She consumes the life of the boy – the "boy" being
  the innate masculinity, the basic identity as male.

And he goes to sleep in paralysis by the loss of
  his potent life.

The widow has some sense of guilt, some idea of her wrong,
  as do all women who kill men.
  "What do you have against me, man of God?
  Did you come to remind me of my sin and kill my son?"
  1 Kings 17:18 NIV

  Once again her solution is relinquishment.
  Elijah said, "Give me your son."

He was "her son," her property for her use.
  Such ownership suffocates the boy in a man.

The woman must give up her hold over a man,
  but the man also must gain back his male soul.
The Elijah-nature of God comes to bring this about.

  "He took him from her arms, carried him
  to the upper room where he was staying
  and laid him on his bed."
  1 Kings 17:19 NIV

Then this virile prophet – with all the fire and courage
of masculinity ignited by knowing God –
began to pray.

*"Then he stretched himself out on the boy
three times and cried to the Lord...
and the boy's life returned to him and
he lived."*
1 Kings 17:21,22 NIV

Intense prayer, impassioned commitment,
personal involvement – these are the
divine powers of the Elijah-anointing to
raise manhood from the grave
of Jezebel annihilation!

Three is the number of completion –
Elijah would stay until life came back,
whatever that required of
his own personal sacrifice.
Only life would do. Only resurrection.

Elijah is the spirit of intercession.
Fervent impassioned prayer.
The very energy of the Holy Spirit desiring
God's purpose to reign.

Relinquishment to God and resurrection by prayer –
these were the weapons Elijah discovered
in Zarephath to defeat the Jezebel-Ahab
scheme of God's Diabolical Enemy.

Elijah had served the time of "small beginnings."
He had been faithful just to obey
and care about the *one.*

Elijah was primed now to face the big battle…

Tolerating Jezebel

"Nevertheless I have this against you:
You tolerate that woman Jezebel
who calls herself a prophetess."
Revelation 2:20,22

Jezebel is the name of Satan given
    to evil of the Last Days.
She must be overcome by every believer.

To tolerate her is to incur God's opposition
and worse, His scathing judgment in real suffering.

To "tolerate" is the failure to object to something
    in opposition to your values.
It is a weakness of character, making you an
      accomplice to evil when all you meant to do
      was merely stay out of the way of
        Jezebel-rage.

To tolerate her is to become an Ahab,
      the failure to take her on in
      all her dreadful power and stare her down.
      Just let her be – let her have her way –
      and you will be punished with the actual agony of
        sickness and trouble.

34

"I will cast her upon a bed of sickness
and those who commit adultery
with her into great tribulation..."

Revelation 2:22

Every believer will meet Jezebel.
Satan's Jezebel-scheme is to intimidate you
    into a corner of
    mute compliance with infamy.

    Jezebel comes in the form of father, mother, sister,
        brother – spouse – even Christian friend.
    It is Jezebel you meet. Not flesh and blood,
        but a principality and power whose
        goal is to quench your "no"
        and steal your God.

When you can no longer object to what oppresses you,
    when your "no" is silenced and
    even your heart accepts the loss of your volition,
    then you have given Jezebel reign over you and
        it will be a *reign of terror* by deliberate fear.

To acquiesce to Jezebel is to sleep with the Enemy
        and leave your Shepherd's shadow.
    To bring you back,
        He will awaken you by the rod of His Pure Correction
        and show you He is more to be
        feared than the Tyrant.

Or He will woo you by the cords of love and prove
to you He is worth the fight for freedom.

And to survive, you will have to recover your "no,"
and shout it to your own ear.
In the end it isn't Jezebel you must overcome,
but the covert trembling of your own heart
in the face of her raging.

When Jezebel is allowed to besiege you,
over all of it is the
One with Blazing Eyes
who wants to destroy your
yellow streak of cowardice.

Sold To Jezebel

Ahab said to Elijah, 'So you have found me, my enemy?'
'I have found you,' he answered, 'because you have sold
yourself to do evil in the sight of the LORD.'

1 Kings 21:20

"There was no one like Ahab, who sold himself to do
wickedness in the sight of the LORD,
urged on by Jezebel his wife."

1 Kings 21:25

Where there is "Jezebel", there is always "Ahab."
This has to be so for Jezebel to dominate.
Only Ahab makes it possible for her to rule
by the absence of his "no."

There is a sense in which we are all Ahabs to Satan's Jezebel.
Compliance with wrong and compromise of integrity
are the weaknesses that invite the Ahab-spirit
of acquiescence to the Jezebel-principality.

Ahabs do not sell their **souls** to Satan – "Ahab sold **himself.**"
His entire being, soul and body, mind and will,
given over to Jezebel by a deliberate act for
which God held him totally accountable.

Remember, Jezebel is about ownership…
lands, kingdoms, but also souls.
Especially souls… of men and women…

And an unspoken contract is entered:
"I give you (Satan) my 'self' and
    you give me something I desire more than
      my own existence."
    It's a bargain made with hell and
    will take you there.

An Ahab person-in-weakness assumes
    if he/she gives the responsibility for life
    to another that the burden is off and
    the answer to God can be: it's not my fault.

But God holds you accountable for what
    you allow to take you over.

There is no escape from accountability before the Father
    who gave you the precious gift of responsibility.
The fearful and the lazy hate responsibility
    and delude themselves that it can be skirted.

Adam and Eve were given a work to do even before the fall.
Responsibility is a privilege and the adventure of growth.
    But the weak and the fearful will invite the Ahab-spirit
    of compliance and give the rule to Jezebel…
      to wiggle out of duty.

Ahab wanted Naboth's vineyard, apparently a prime piece of
    land the man's family had developed for generations.
    Ahab wouldn't commit to the work of building
       a similar treasure. He wanted someone else's
    flourishing garden without the digging.   (21:3)
        He demanded the fruit of another's labor.
           This is the Ahab-spirit.

Unwilling to pay the price that Naboth had paid,
    Ahab took to his lazy bed in the
        depression of self pity.   (21:4)

When greed meets laziness, Satan is there in the form
    of someone with the Jezebel evil who promises
       to bear your load so you don't have to,
       to provide your desires and serve you.
    And that one will do so with a strange
       absence of basic integrity.

Ahab's intense fear motivated his weakness.
       The fruit of that fear: dread of responsibility
       and hatred for duty.
    It is easier to let the industrious have the reins.
       Or so it seems…

    But it will cost you!
       That objective of greed
         with consent to laziness
         will cost your very life.

This amounts to a contract with Satan,
binding and absolute, that can only be canceled
by repentance for rebellion
in a broken spirit.

Ahab could blame Jezebel for obtaining what he wanted –
he could be innocent of the murder.

But the prophet brought God's mind and
held Ahab accountable for
letting Jezebel entice him.

Ahab lost his throne, his favor with God, his place in
Divine History, and ultimately his life.
He lived by cowardice and died the same,
still hiding behind a disguise,   (22:30)
refusing to be the king God had made him.

He was sentenced to die in exact likeness to Jezebel,
by the gruesome devouring of dogs. (22:38)

Our volition is intact and cannot be captured.
Sacred choice can only be given away, never seized,
and when that is done deliberately,
it is selling-yourself-to-do-evil.

The evil he allowed Jezebel to do was attributed
to him. In the end, he didn't escape from any
responsibility.
God accepts no excuse, even if we do.

The Almighty places each person in the arena of an assignment
by His Sovereign Knowledge of what He created in us.
We are fitted for the task by design
and equipped for its fulfillment
through *need of Him* to explain it
and His power to perform it.

All this He waits to do with unending willingness.
He equips us with a need, deep and voracious,
but not with a strength that would make us independent.

He stands ready to bear our load
if we will only shoulder it... first.

Since all is provided, no excuse will be accepted and
no blame of another tolerated.

"... each of us will give an account of himself to God."
Romans 14:12

God reckons the evil-of-weakness to be equal to
the evil-of-tyranny and gives the
same consequences to both.
If you support tyranny by the failure
to fight it,
you *are* the tyrant!

Jezebel's Teaching

*"calls herself a prophetess [claiming to be inspired], and
who is teaching and leading astray my servants and
beguiling them into practicing
sexual vice and eating food sacrificed to idols."*
Rev. 2:20 Amplified Bible

Jezebel appoints herself, seizes a lofty spiritual position
    not ordained by heaven.
Claiming to represent that place
    from which she has been expelled and rejected,
    she alleges to speak for God… as God!

Do not think Jezebel lives only in the barroom of vice.
The ultimate Jezebel-spirit is a religious zealot,
    driven by a mad ambition to be religiously superior
    to everyone, especially the genuine.

Religious by a grandiosity she conjures up around herself.
    Lying goodness. Words only. And no reality.

She was passionate to create many prophets for
    the idol of *her choice.*
She relished the hunt and kill of God's true spokesmen.

Jezebel is the principality of **False Religion,**
    using God while hating Him.
    She takes things spiritual for her own promotion,
        creates mystical lies, and feigns worship.
Masquerades as a believer and even names God.

But she doesn't mean the Heavenly Father, the Creator.
She serves another spirit being, an Invisible Monster,
and he is her Veiled Master.

Jezebel was the entity behind the Pharisees of
Jesus' displeasure.
He had no hesitation to name the power
behind their arrogance.
"You are of your Father the devil."

Jezebel is the "spirit of religion," and
the method of her proselyting is seduction.

She is beguiling.
With brilliant persuasion she pulls down your values and
standards until she achieves a compromise with
lusts of the flesh by which she would shackle you...

She is the quintessential snake.
By velvet flattery,
she will coax and preach in defense of your pleasure.

She dulls the sharp edge of your integrity
by her cold stone of relentless pressure.

Jezebel uses arguments to the mind,
evil spirits to bombard the soul,
and enticements to the eye.

These are the creeds of her religion:
Her god is Baal, the sexual god of debauchery;
    The worship of "feeling good" by the
        satiating of whatever craving comes to mind.
        Should you bond with her,
    she will take you to that temple of sordid worship
        by any route she can find.

Behind sexual obsession, eating disorders, and drug abuse
lurks this queen of flesh, Jezebel.
        Until her reign is destroyed,
    escape from those prisons is elusive.
Wherever flesh is out of control – raving with appetite –
        there you will find the Jezebel spirit
            in clandestine control.

Immorality has many back roads of compromise
        other than sex.
And she uses them all with no remorse.

Accusation. Greed for gain. Unscrupulous ambition.
Murder. Lying. Slander.
    You can find these: her methods
        and her motives in the story.

Her "teaching" shreds you in a way so devious
    you cannot prove her malice.
It leaves you mindless, confused by her overpowering logic,
        without an answer… without a "self."
        In the extreme, the tirade of her words
            makes you feel almost insane.

The one-in-Jezebel is never wrong and
doesn't have to bow so low as a simple apology.

There is no influencing her... there is no changing her.
She will not be restrained.

You cannot survive a person in Jezebel by extending friendship.
She demands an intimacy that rapes your soul.

You have to flee for your life.
If you can't flee, at least don't let her hold your hand.
And above all, don't listen to Jezebel.
Her so-called "teaching" is an invitation to hell.

Only the prophetic spirit of Elijah can deal with her.
Speak and flee.

Confront and run to God.
Call down fire and pray for rain.

Mount Carmel

Counterfeit religion has neither power nor fire.
Divine Might rains and reigns with both!

Troubler of Israel

"And it came to pass after many days that
the word of the Lord came to Elijah, in the third year:
'Go, present yourself to Ahab, and
I will send rain on the earth.'
So Elijah went to present himself to Ahab."
1 Kings 18:1,2

Elijah came out of hiding...
you have to hide your spirit from the one-in-Jezebel...
and only speak when the Word of the Lord comes to you.

It takes time alone with God – much time alone –
    to penetrate the Jezebel force,
        to be free of the demonic clouds of confusion.
        To **hear**.

Elijah waited three years to get that single Word.
He wouldn't move without it.

All the while Elijah looked for God, Ahab was looking for him.

Understand that the Jezebel-Ahab spirit hounds the prophet;
    is always searching for the prophet with murder in mind.

The rain stands for the blessing of God on a land
    and the symbol of His presence.
He wanted to end judgment and send rain but not until
    the **satanic worship of flesh** was destroyed.

Elijah did not go directly to Jezebel, nor to Ahab
    to begin the destruction of their reign.
He went after the false gods that ruled her –
       the spiritual power behind the human power.

God sets His order in the universe by Divine Government.
Mankind has its officials…
    humanity presides by the election of itself,
    but God has His own rulers of nations!
And their authority is greater than any strutting despot.

When Elijah appeared from the place of hiding
    in God's presence,
Ahab asked, "Is that you, O Troubler of Israel?" (1 Kings 18:17)

Ahab was king, directing armies and executioners.
But Elijah was quicksilver, immune to mere human rule.
    He couldn't be found.
    He wouldn't be killed.

Ahab was the real problem for God's nation –
Elijah, troubling to Ahab's Jezebel-influenced goal:
      the total destruction of God-worship.
That was the real trouble,
      and Elijah was set to untrouble Israel.

When you trouble the king of your country, you have
    more authority than the king.
God Almighty can supersede any monarch
    by His own reign and
    His people – by His appointment – are to rule rulers.

God's endorsement of a prophet to a time and place is
    unmovable… and untouchable.

The realm of humanity is ruled by chaos and accident,
but the Divine Realm – the Kingdom of Heaven –
has its complete order.
    That order of the Kingdom,
        the unseen realm, actually rules over earth
        when God can secure a willing vessel to
            bear His mantle of leadership.

Heaven rules –
if just one lone person will let heaven rule him/her.
The Kingdom of Heaven is a realm
    of complete and peaceful order
    by the Absolute Authority of our Eternal King.
Heaven's pattern invades the earth only through
    the administration of God's authority…
                resting on a human vessel.

War against evil is all about authority, not struggle.
    Evil bows only to authority… to nothing else.
Humanity must choose to bow. Free will is his gift.
    But the forces of darkness have to surrender
        when God-derived authority is
            in action.

Elijah bore the authority of a Divine Commission
    so he could challenge the vile prophets of Baal
        to a duel of fire.

Elijah didn't take on Jezebel, nor did he fight Ahab.
He was a prophet and only a prophet can defeat a prophet.
It takes a king to defeat a king. It would take King Jehu to
finally topple Jezebel. Elijah didn't attempt to take her on.

Victory is an authority issue... only *authority* wins.

Elijah, as a man of absolute obedience,
    knew the limits of his assignment
      and stayed within them.
This is the Elijah-anointing.
John the Baptist had it also,
      declared himself to be only... the Voice.
      No more than that.

So Elijah took on the prophets of Baal and destroyed them.
He had a God-anointed sanction for that.
He undermined the queen by destroying her idols.
      The power behind the power.

He could mock the god of the Baals because
      he knew his own Almighty.
Elijah knew who was really God
    by letting the True One be God over... himself.

Rebellion has no power over rebellion.
Elijah's surrender empowered him with Divine Commitment
      proven in his answered prayers.

Standing as one lonely prophet against 450
      plus all the citizens who watched,
Elijah was the man-in-charge
      orchestrating the fire of heaven.

But everything he did was by Divine instruction,
      specific and detailed...
      down to the last drop of water.
All given by a secret commission through abject surrender.

> *"I am Your servant and I have done all these things*
> *at Your word."*
> 1 Kings 18:36

A man under authority knows his sphere of power.
He uses it to the full,
      but never steps over his permission from Heaven.
He operates in – believes in –
      no authority proceeding out of his own arrogance,
      but serves only as the emissary of Another's Dominion.

Listen to the mighty prayer of Elijah.
He didn't command God, nor order fire.
He prayed for God to perform His promise
      to His willing servant.

Elijah's power was not of fire. That was God's power.
Elijah's personal power was in prayer based on
      his hard-won knowledge of God's wishes.

And he prayed by fervor and passion for
      the God he loved to be vindicated by His own actions –

        "O Lord... let it be known this day that
            you are God in Israel."

He prayed by persistence that would not stop short of realization,

        "Hear me O Lord, hear me..."

Elijah won over rebellion
by the power of his concealed obedience.
By ruling only in the arena of impassioned prayer.

The power of God resting on a prophet
      lies in two elements, both unseen...
One is the very private bow of absolute surrender
      to the Only God.

The other is the knowledge of His will and
      the understanding that where His will assigns you,
      there is your sphere of winning authority...

Absolute Rule by virtue of... ***abject surrender...***

The Fire of Heaven
1 Kings 18

Elijah was sent to defeat Jezebel, but that
wasn't his featured goal, only the offshoot.
It was simply sweeping the house clean for
    the arrival of the King.

Elijah's real mission was the restoration of
    the Glorious God to His rightful place.
    And for His chosen people to see it.

*"O Lord, God of Abraham, Isaac, and Israel,
let it be known this day that **you are God in Israel**."*
verse 36 NKJ (Emphasis mine)

To focus on evil is to become like
    the evil of your concentration,
        to end up equal to the evil you hate.
        Or worse.

Evil is not the centrality of the universe.
The tyranny of Satan is false rule,
    operating now only on
    an illegitimate basis.

Satan must be empowered by your faith in his power.
    Without that, he is hollow and helpless.
Satan taunts to get you in a tussle with him,
and by this struggle to conquer him, pin you in unbelief.
Daring confidence-by-faith is to walk away as
    the declared winner.

The many prophets of Baal could raise
    not one faint spark of power for their altar.

A vivid picture of Satan's real level of powerlessness
    in the face of one who knows the Genuine God.

Elijah was blazing with God
    in behalf of His vindication and exaltation!

"Hear me, O Lord, hear me, that
this people may know that you are the Lord God
and that you have turned their hearts back to You again."
    verse 37 NKJ

The fire of God burned in Elijah and
    its spark ignited Heaven-sent flames
    so great that even the stones were burned,
    gallons of water were "licked up," and
    even the soil under the altar consumed.

The Elijah-zeal roared across Mount Carmel
    down to a massive slaughter in the Kishon Valley
        of God's enemies.
    Some, slain by Elijah himself.

That fierce passion – that unmatchable energy –
    was motivated more by a fervent love for God,
    than merely a burning hatred of Baal.

By that fearless intensity in defense of God, evil was slain.
And the throne of Jezebel began to totter.

The judgment of God had fallen by Elijah's flaming prayer.
Israel was free from the veil of evil seduction –
free to recognize God's Face again.

And that was his goal!

Abundance of Rain

"And Elijah said to Ahab, 'Go, eat and drink,
for there is the sound of an abundance of rain.'"
1 Kings 18:41

Elijah could hear heaven's plans for earth.
He could hear the rush of rain in the middle of drought.

O, to hear as Elijah! To hear the sounds of reality, of
God's graceful showers, ready to pour out!
To see the rain in heaven before it hits the clouds!

Elijah was a man of keen hearing,
tuned in precision to
the frequency of Another Realm.

Elijah spent more time listening than speaking.
The mark of his life was living
inside God's Great Imagination
where the strange and wonderful are conceived.

His hearing was honed by the intense focus of long waiting
in the silence of every human voice, including his own.

He heard drought and he heard rain –
both judgment and benediction,
the full range of God.

His hearing was not selective to his own agenda,
　　nor dulled by obvious sights of the unreal.
His ear was surrendered and void of opinion,
　　tuned to a Voice above the fray,
　　　　speaking the only-real-truth that
　　　　dwells beyond the present sky.

So in the weary drought, in the thirst of desperation,
　　Elijah heard —
　　　　not just rain — but *abundance* of rain.

The God of Twelve-Baskets-left-over,
　　waiting in His limitless generosity
　　　　for the justice of Baal's defeat,
　　was gathering water together, ready to pour.

And Elijah heard the gushing.

Heaven is full of joyful sounds.
　　The shout of victory,
　　the trumpet of judgment,
　　the song of jubilation.

And over all,
the Great Creative Voice of God like
　　　　the roar of rushing floods.

Who can hear heaven?
Who can bring the sounds of that far-off realm
    into this loud world,
        void of holy resonance,
        empty of lovely silence?
It takes an Elijah-anointing of detachment
    from racket and lie...
    the honed skill of listening,
    deliberately deaf to the vacant flap of
        God's enemy...
    to hear heaven's ring.

Sound comes before appearance.
Somewhere there has to be one who hears
    the Divine Rustling and calls forth the appearance
    of that which resonates in heaven.

There was yet no thunder. No cloud.
    But so sure was Elijah of the sound of rain
        in the ear of his spirit,
            that he announced its certain coming.

Travail of Rain

*"Go, eat and drink, for there is the sound of
a heavy rain."*

Elijah, commander of fire and kings, ordered his enemy
to eat and drink. And he went!

Imagine Ahab's shock with his prophets strewn
across the Kishon valley, slain by the very subjects of
his own kingdom – at the direction of Elijah, that troubler.
Even an enemy-king would obey such a frightening
man of God! *"So Ahab went off to eat and drink."*

*"Elijah climbed to the top of Mount Carmel,
bent down to the ground and
put his face between his knees."*

The mountain is always the symbol of meeting God,
the place of intimate prayer.
High and above the world,
remote and alone: this is prayer.
This is prayer.

Prayer is birthing.
Having conceived the secret of God in
a private tryst with Him,
hearing His vital seed and
nurturing it with time until it is so certain,
so imminent,
it cannot be kept hidden any longer.

Taking the birthing position,
    Elijah began to travail for his vision.

As in all delivery, at first there was nothing.
The strain and effort brought no rain, not so much as a cloud.
The servant, sent to watch, reported, "nothing there."

But Elijah was seized now by the heavings of the Spirit
    to bring God's will to earth.

When prayer is this intense it is
    beyond the human and into
        the unquenchable desire of God.

He seeks for a servant so committed to His will –
to His wishes – that prayer can rise into the level
    of the Lord's impassioned power.
        And that brings an endurance, superhuman and effective.

It wasn't just water falling on parched crops and thirsty cattle.
    The rain was a cleansing flood of God's very life,
        poured out in grace on a people,
        soiled by vile worship of the god of sex.

A people who didn't deserve it, but so desperately needed it.
A people who had preferred bondage to freedom;
        a defaming idol to the Real God.

God Almighty longed for His people
        so He spent long years
        in the careful training of one solitary life;

one vessel that could carry… and would endure the very
   agony of a Father who had lost His children.

It wasn't rain. It was a demonstration of God's love,
   His favor, and His unmerited mercy.
It was birthing God back again into the nation.

For such an outpouring,
   the prayer had to be one of deep anguish.
      Not shallow pleasantries.

The one who will birth God's very presence into a
   wretched idolatrous setting
   must be willing to pray
      from the **nothing** to the **appearance**.
      From heaven to earth.
      Seven times: the number of perfection.
        Till it comes…

At last, a tiny indication:
"a cloud as small as a man's hand – rising from the sea,"
   and from that tiny beginning,
   a storm thrashing with rain.

In these Last Days,
Baal rises again to lure the children
   away from their Pure Father,
      into bondage of the flesh – sordid and base –
lost in a madness of obsession with sex and food.

And the Good Father yearns with wailing agony
for His captured sheep.

He will seek for one who stands with Him on the mountain.
The Lord will carefully prepare these Last-Day-Elijahs
by secret training in the villages of
widows and dying boys.

And He will fill that man or woman
with an Elijah-heart of the brooding Fatherhood of God.

That Final Elijah will fiercely carry the torch of
God's true identity as Father
to a whole generation of the fatherless and childless,
and they *will be restored.*

And prayer will take on the birthing position again:
Elijah travailing for the latter rain
of God's merciful presence
to bathe His errant children from Jezebel's filthy gods.

Running With God

"Then the hand of the Lord came upon Elijah;
and he girded up his loins and
ran ahead of Ahab to the entrance of Jezreel."

The palace of Jezebel was in the valley of Jezreel.
Ahab drove his chariot in her direction when the rain began,
    taking his orders from his enemy.

Elijah said,
"Go and tell Ahab, 'Hitch up your chariot
and go down before the rain stops you.'"
1 Kings 18:46

Elijah ran beside the chariot of Ahab,
    so empowered by God's energy that he went ahead
        of the horses and arrived at Jezreel first!

Human feet pitted against the flying hooves of many horses.
And the race covered many miles where
    only horse-strength could endure.

Such a race has never been won, before or since.

The "Zeal of the Lord of Hosts" possessed Elijah
    by his faith in heaven's superiority
        to hell's fraudulent power.

Such a race was entirely supernatural and
    an overflow from the victory on Carmel
        over Baal's soothsayers.

"Energy" is a primary target of Jezebel.
    To sap, drain, and extinguish
        the light of God's Indwelling Spark.

To implant weakness: physical, moral and spiritual.
    That is the demonic Jezebel method of mastery.

But God's Divine Vigor in the arena of
    His fiery confrontation with evil
        was an unstoppable force
    and caught Elijah in its Overpowering Wake.

By fearless confrontation with Baal/Jezebel,
    God surges into your life
    with conquering enthusiasm, a joy of victory
        that energizes your whole being.

This is God's infusion of vitality – and even His reward –
    given to the believer who will challenge Baal head-on.

Wilderness of Fear

Fear of evil is a blank wasteland
far from God's presence, but near
His Watching Love.

Running from Jezebel

If you cease to run **with** God, you will run **from** Jezebel.
And run you must, when Jezebel is in the arena of your life.

Elijah had been dealing with Ahab,
    advising and commanding.

But the Ahab-spirit of cowardice is dangerous and
contagious. To be with an Ahab in any measure is
to be tainted by that nonresistant weakness
    and to experience the awakening of your own
        bent toward faintheartedness.

You have to be against the Ahab-spirit that is
    a fully equal companion to Jezebel-evil.

No sympathy. No fellowship.
Only opposition to that compromising defect.

Elijah, prophet in God's presence, skilled listener to His heart,
    made the deadly mistake of
        hearing Jezebel.
Her death-threat entered his mind and
    froze the fire in his heart.

> *"Elijah was afraid and ran for his life."*
> I Kings 19:3

From Jezreel in the far north of Israel,
    to the southern end of Judah – to Beersheba, he ran.

A very long way.
Still further, another day's journey into the desert…
    he went alone.
    Fear is a desert experience and will take you
        far, far from God.

The Jezebel-spirit operates in violent assault.
By vicious words – or ruthless silence – 'she' brags of her
power. Intending to inflict terrible suffering and dreaming of
murder, the Jezebel-spirit terrorizes the strongest of souls.

Jezebel's tactic of capture is intimidation. Her threats are the
most dreadful she can conjure and are always tinged with the
death of something. Ultimately, it is the consummate death –
spiritual death.

"It" wants you to be involved in the "deep things of Satan."
Endlessly considering him and the secrets of an evil
that pretends to be fascinating.

But the deep knowledge of Satan is forbidden. (Rev. 2:24)
It turns into a torture of fear, a literal nightmare
where voices blitz the mind and God's truth is perverted.

The cruel aggression of Jezebel, bearing an insidious satanic
power, attacked Elijah and he was finally worn down by it.

Every ounce of his being,
– his spiritual power, his physical resources –
had been poured into
    the defeat of darkness.

His life-force was utterly drained in the fight.
   Though the victory was awesome,
   though the win was total,
     he was left with a bone weariness
     that made him vulnerable to the rage of hell.

And Elijah, in the heat of her obscene threat,
   by the weight of her undimmed power,
     was spent and broken.

"Then he lay down under the tree and fell asleep."
I Kings 19:5

Suddenly exhausted by an utter fatigue,
   an abnormal blood-drained weakness
   peculiar to the battle of Jezebel,
     Elijah collapsed.

When Satan-in-Jezebel throws all the force of
   demonic hatred at you, and it lands a mark
     in your vexed soul and weary body,
      the best remedy
     is just the practical cure of rest.

Entirely human, completely understandable…
   if you have met Jezebel, you have moaned
     under the juniper tree.

And I hope you just let yourself sleep.

Elijah's Despair

Jezebel remained on her savage throne.
  The dramatic fire from heaven had not
    so much as scorched her.
  The great victory seemed shallow.
  It had only served to more enrage the evil monarch.

Jezebel had seen the demonstration of God's true power
      overwhelm her idol but
    because she – even then – didn't bow to that True Ruler,
      she was more entrenched than ever
        in her evil realm.

And Elijah, in utter despair, preferred to die
    than exist in the presence of such
    unconquerable evil.

His victory had not discouraged the hateful queen.
  Her murderous nature, only aroused.

"I cannot win! I cannot even try any more.
    And it is unbearable to live in the same world
      with this indomitable evil!"

"It is enough! Now, Lord, take my life." 1 Kings 19:4

In Elijah's view, she had won.
Despite God's display of fire power,
    regardless of the people's choice of their True God,
      Jezebel's reign of terror was intact.

"I have had enough, Lord," he said,
"Take my life. I am no better than my ancestors."
I Kings 19:4

More than a sense of failure overwhelmed him.
He had not conquered her, and he also faced the
   real fact that he could not defeat her.

It was not only that he failed,
   it was that **he could not win.**

Elijah's weakness tortured him.
He stood helpless against an evil he was assigned to conquer.
Despite the defeat of her "religion,"
     the humiliating demise of her prophets,
     Jezebel was undaunted
her rage and evil, more rampant than ever.

What was the good of defeating the prophets of Baal?
She remained triumphant and unstopped.

Elijah was to learn that he had not failed,
   but it *was* true that he could not win.

Elijah had vast authority over the demonic realm.
   He commanded all the elements of nature
     through his fervent prayer:
     drought, rain, and fire from heaven!

   He could call the people to a choice
   and free them from Satan's hold.

He could literally murder hell's power
     held by Jezebel and
destroy the false religion that had
     captivated the nation.
Such power! Such dominion!

But he could not conquer the willful, egocentric
     rebellion of a stiff-necked human being.
     He couldn't change a person
who was given by continuing choice
     to deliberate evil.

He had no authority nor fire power,
     no potent prayer that could stop the
     rampant stubborn will of a
person so wildly intent on being
     an embodiment of Satan.

Jezebel was cold steel, unmeltable
     even by Elijah's great fire of God.
     And he knew it.

His despair was not the cowering of a weak man.
It was the courageous facing of a grim reality.
     He had come to the end of his power
     and authority.
     And he recognized he had no ability
to destroy Jezebel, nor her defiant throne.

His understandable fatigue was joined
to legitimate despair, and the
only escape from such unconquerable wickedness
seemed to be... death.

His desire for death was an instinctive solution.
It was not Elijah who should die,
but his concept of God,
now outdated and obsolete.

And it would take a long process by
the Father's patient nurture
before Elijah could comprehend
the amazing secret to evil's destruction.

Cake and Coals

*"Suddenly an angel touched him and said,
'Arise and eat.' He looked, and there by his head was
a cake baked on coals and a jar of water.
So he ate and drank and lay down again."*
1 Kings 19:5,6

In the beginning of Elijah's journey, God sent ravens and meat.
Water flowed from the brook beside him.
Provision out of earth, the common elements.

But now the aid is from another realm.
No intervening agent of raven or widow.
The supply is straight from heaven.
In this time of desperation and hunger,
it is an angel and the appearance of
supernatural bread
baked fresh over hot coals.
Water where there was no water.
All from heaven, no more earthly food.

Bread stands for the living appearance of the Lord.
No longer meat with ruminating work to do,
but **bread**: the life-giving presence of the Lord,
our most basic necessity.
Not merely bread, but *bread from heaven*.
Fresh for the NOW-need of Elijah's today.

And water from a jar, where no wilderness-water flowed.
Water, the cleansing power of God's Voice.
As water flushes the body, the Word cleans
    the *soul* from the stain and injury of
    the filthy war with Jezebel.

A war more vicious than any human battle
    by the unchecked lawlessness
      of the enemy's evil.

Hot coals of comfort are the healing balm of the Lord.
When God makes a holy fire for your sustenance –
    as Jesus did for Peter on the shore –
    it is for the healing of
      terrible memories, shameful failure and
      fearful nightmares.

The fire of judgment upon idolatry is one thing.
The gentle glow of coals, sent to warm your soul's chill,
    is the fire of the Father's nurture.

God's presence with God's voice:
      this is the ravaged soul's entire healing,
    the amazing transformation of having God find you
      by His ministering angel…

Though Elijah ran in the fantasy of fear,
    God's eye had followed him
      to the barren desert of his panic
        and by tender mercy, nurtured His prophet…
      even there.

Angel, bread, water and hot coals: symbols of the
      direction of Elijah's path, of what God had in mind
         for his future experience.

But before the man could take hold of his future,
      he had to leave the hiding place of his fright.
    And this required a twice-fed rest,
       a deep and profound sleep,
         the restoration of his aching body and bruised soul,
           a respite from the "war of lies,"
  and the resolving of the lie Elijah had swallowed –
  a lie that made him leave the surety of His God.

    For now the bread and water were
      merely a symbol of the promise.
    Elijah had yet to hear
      the Voice and know the Awesome Presence.

The manifestation of God – His gifts and angels –
      is not the same as
         the presence of God.

His actual Presence is in another place…
      and much to be preferred.

Lies of Jezebel

Jezebel has two lies: one, that you need her.
  The other, you cannot conquer her.

Jezebel will convince you her dictatorship is actually love,
    and her purpose is your fulfillment.
      This she did to Ahab.

She touts her worth. In subtle form she says,
      "You cannot make it without me."
        Take this inside and you are an instant Ahab.

"You are dependent on me and without me
    you will be lost.
    You will know nothing.
    You will have nothing.
      Only with my sanction can you be a success,
      but… if you leave me I will kill you.
    With me you will live, without me you will die."

  The doubly bolted door of her prison…
  the promise for staying and the threat if you leave.

The lie is that she is god… a two-sided lie:
    She is source and she is power.

You cannot fear unless you swallow the lie that
    God is weaker than Jezebel.

When you discover her villainy and want to escape,
the lie of Jezebel's conceit is this: she always wins
     by a power so evil and so potent
       that even God cannot conquer it.

"God cannot master me." The convincing Lie of Jezebel
     and "You will never get away from me."
Jezebel sends this delusion to the Elijah-prophet.
   By a deafening noise of boasting,
     in the threat of god-like power,
       she poses as one who rules life and death,
      and swears to *your death.*

It registers as terrifyingly real – "she can actually do it."
    And the best of God's servants cringe before it.

The recovery of the prophet's faith demands the
    dispelling of all the heinous lies,
and Father God, by tender ministrations,
   will see to it through the
     revelation of... *Himself.*

Weakness and Courage

There are two kinds of weakness.

One is the weakness of Ahab.
> The lack of valor, a shirking of duty.
> A cowardice that flees from
> > the slightest show of any pompous strength.
> An unwillingness to fight or even to work...
> and above all, fear of man, and
> > an absence of reverence for God.

The other is the weakness of Elijah.
One who is intent on obedience,
> fierce for God's interest...
> who will face his calling and
> > move toward it with all his heart.

But the faithful will – without exception – meet
> the collapse of human power to effect divine purposes.

Weakness is the human condition, whether
> weakness of the gutless,
> or weakness of the ardent.

Living with the *awareness of human weakness,*
> in the presence of a zealous heart for God,
> > takes enormous courage...

The only remedy for Elijah was communion with
the Source of Strength, his Real Father.
By that intimate contact,
Elijah was infused with God's own power.
True spiritual might is *imparted* not achieved
and not possible to normal humanity.

"Ahab" is merely weakness-accepted and fear-pampered.

Weakness must be grieved over, mourned, and regretted.
Helplessness must be acknowledged
in gut-wrenching truth,
but in this salient paradox... hated as unacceptable.

And the anguish of powerlessness and limitation is
the very energy to solve it.
Grief and despair over spiritual poverty is the
excruciating drive toward the prayer that is
the solution: God's infused power.

In the Hebrews list of heroes who *"shut the mouths of lions,*
quenched the fury of the flames and
escaped the edge of the sword"
were those very human people
"whose weakness was turned to strength."
Heb. 11:33,34 NIV

Weakness is no obstacle. It is merely a test.
The choice is this: will you be an Ahab or an Elijah?
The potential of both directions lies within us, **all** of us.
How you face your own secret weakness will determine it.

The Kingdom *does* belong to the poor.
Comfort is the solace to those who mourn in pain;
and holiness, the Divine Award *given* to those with
the courage to be weak… and thirsty.

Matt. 5:3,4,6

Recovering God's Will

"… and he went in the strength of that food forty days
and forty nights as far as Horeb,
the mountain of God."
1 Kings 19:8

Elijah chose to hide in the desert,
    a place that pictured his desolation.
But the place of his belonging was the mountain,
    and to that high place he had to return.

God is on the mountain, a realm above
    the scorch of earth's fallenness.

    Though He ministers to you in Sheol,
        He communes with you only on the mountain.

The prophet can live only if he lives from the mountain;
his abiding home must be in those lonely heights,
    no matter where his feet may wander.

Elijah had left the mountain-dwelling
    for the wilderness of common terror.
He had to make the journey-of-return assisted by
        God's agents and even a
power given *by* God to make the journey.

The mountain of Elijah's calling was no longer
    the Carmel of his past victories.

When you have destroyed the idolatry underneath Jezebel,
   you go up to a different field of God's purpose.

He was called to Mt. Horeb, another name for Sinai,
   the mountain of Moses, of smoke and fire,
     of the terror of God and His holy law.

Though Elijah believed his victory ended in defeat,
God's view was to promote this faithful man
   to a higher level of authority.
Of this, Elijah had no clue,
   being caught in the mind set of Jezebel's lie –
     the boast of her illicit power.

So two hundred miles he traveled in a direction south, entirely
   opposite to the northern Mt. Carmel of his familiarity.

When you have left God's will, you have left God.
   And the journey back can be long, but is sustained
     by God's impassioned strength for the travel.
       He stoops to help you recover His purpose
       when Jezebel has driven you from it.

Fasting for forty days and nights,
   Elijah's weakness increased, but his panic quieted.
   Fasting is self-imposed death, starvation of the
     craving soul.
   Errant emotion and false urgency needed to die,
     not the man himself.
   Fasting conquers those fleshly lusts of fear.

Elijah, possessed now only by the strength of God –
    only by the Divine Energy to obey
      His direction and return to His will.

God had all along prepared a hiding place for Elijah
    better than the wilderness, safer than its exposure
      to the demonic cries that dwell there.

It was a cave of God's arranging,
    inside the mountain of His law.
A place that neither Jezebel nor her demonic agents
    would dare approach.

God's will is safety. God's will is a haven.
    And Jezebel is intent on driving you from God's will,
    screaming loudly by frightening intimidation
      when you buck her.
    Or by soothing flattery when you let her rule.
      You can lose your path in the confusing noise
      of her never-ending aggression.

The God Who is All will send help to the desert,
    but He waits in the place of
      His will for you to come to Him.

He is God.
He will bow to no terms other than His own.
    He condescends to help, but He never leaves
      His purpose or His dominion.

By the Divine Patience of His Omnipresence,
      God waits…
   and He waits, unmoving and uncompromising…
      He mercifully endures
         His frail sheep. This can only come from Love.

"There he went into a cave and
spent the night"

In the center of God's will, you can find the immunity of
   His complete and perfect provision for your safety.
He knows the human shaking before the hellish Jezebel.
   He is the strength of the soul and its hiding place.

Mount Horeb

The Obedient hear a Gentle God
even in the scene of His Terrifying Might.

The Question

*"And the word of the Lord came to him:
'What are you doing here, Elijah?'"*
1 Kings 19:9

God is above all a Father.
   He would have us unmask and name our
      most terrible quandary... to Him.

Elijah had swallowed his crisis and
choked on its introspective poison.
He had tried a self-serving escape
      and that had brought only more dreadful isolation.
His only companions: tormenting lies that
      screamed at him in the wild desert.

It was Eve's mistake, an eternal one,
      to fail to talk to God.
Just talk to Him, that is enough.

When Elijah found his way back to the place of God's provision
      into the arena of His specific will,
      then he could meet with God Himself.

Elijah would find that his cemented opinion was all wrong,
      but he had to bring the error to the Father
   in a straightforward complaint before it could be diffused.

And the Gracious Father coaxed it out of the man
      by the probe of a question.

Elijah's answer was the whine of self-pity.

> *"so he said, "I have been very zealous for*
> *the Lord God Almighty.*
> *The children of Israel have rejected*
> *Your covenant, torn down Your altars and*
> *Killed your prophets with the sword.*
> *I alone am left; and they seek to take my life."*

God Almighty can conquer any foe,
    especially the delusions of the human heart.

But He has to possess the problem by means
    of simple communication.

    Tell God in naked honesty.
    That's all. Just tell Him.
    Then what?
    Nothing.

To tell Him is to give it to Him.
    To tell Him is to open *yourself* to
    the Only Solution… **God**.

When you unveil the dilemma of your heart
    to the Waiting Father –
    simply talking to Him –
He will answer with the whisper of His secret purpose
and restore you completely to your place in His Plan.

Mountain of Law

"Then the Lord said to him...
anoint Hazael,
anoint Jehu... and Elisha."

1 Kings 19:15,16

Elijah, blind by the crushing of Jezebel
had yet to see God's view.

In destroying idolatry,
by having confronted God's people to restore them,
Elijah had been promoted.

He viewed it as defeat... the Lord, as success.
For Elijah had completed the assignment;
carried out God's purposes.
Through prayer, by confrontation,
in the solidity of his faith,
Elijah had simply, but fully obeyed.

And though Elijah wasn't pleased with the
unfinished result, the Lord was.

From his mountain solitude,
God would give him a new commission,
that of anointing and appointing kings.

The Lord ever takes us higher,
but only by steps of devoted obedience
to His specific will.

Elijah was finished warring in the valleys and
    fighting from the mountain of Carmel's hiding.

He who appoints kings and prophets is a ruler,
    no longer a fighter.
Elijah had reached a life in the heavenlies,
    privy to Divine Directives.

No longer wrestling with the "problem" on earth,
Elijah now entered the counsels of
        the Most High God for His purposes in the future,
        His triumph from Above.

Jezebel must be defeated from this realm,
        from God's Indomitable Throne
        where no one can oppose Him
        and survive.

Elijah had moved from Carmel to Horeb.
        Carmel was the place of prayer,
        also hiding and fighting.
        But Horeb – or Sinai – was the place of
        God's blazing dominion
        where the fire of His heavenly throne
        met earth and killed whoever
        touched it without holiness.

To execute God's will on earth by faithful warring
is to eventually come to dwell inside
heaven's Vast Ideas and Purposes,
there to see the course of God's victory
over the enemies of His rule.

The one who commissions rulers of nations
is one who lives in the realm of
heaven's full dominion over all that is this world.

And there, by heaven's absolute order under God,
to rest in the sure and sovereign conquest
of any crowing dictator.

God always has His plan for the defeat of Jezebel,
a long term but certain end of her lawless power.
But that agenda is known by going –
only by Divine invitation –
to the place
of its certainty: His Throne of Flame.

Though Elijah had run away from God's will
to the desert of terror,
he was judged as faithful
by his consistency in obedience.
He was – despite that slip – a lawful man…

God's Law will prevail from Sinai.
    His everlasting Holiness will – in the end –
    be utterly fulfilled.
Elijah had lived under the absolute Law of
    God's personal will for him.
    He was lawful –
        Jezebel, the epitome of the lawless.

Only God can deal with the human arrogance
    that seizes His dominion.

And in that secret to the defeat of Jezebel,
he would discover the God of heaven and earth...

Winds and Earthquakes

God's new command of recovery:

"Go out, and stand on the mountain before the Lord."

Face God. "Go out" of your cowering and
        reckon with Him.
Confront His meeting of *you*!
Stand there and let Him reveal Himself.
Not just His "agenda" but... Himself.

To be in His will is to come to *know* Him,
        and to *know* Him is the goal of His will.

The Elijah-mission is fatherhood.
And to bring that to pass requires an
experience of the Real Father, the "Father of Lights"
in whom there is no fault and no shadow.
And to be personally "Fathered" by the staff of
        His Perfect Correction.

The education of God as Father must hold the
        experience of fearing Him...
        fearing Him more than Jezebel
    by the recognition of His Real power
    contrasted to her meaningless threats.

Fear of God.
This is the void in Jezebel that makes her Jezebel.

Elijah left the cave of his safety to bravely
witness a demonstration of the dominion of
    the One who Rules All.

"And behold, the Lord passed by, and
a great and strong wind tore into the mountains
and broke the rocks in pieces before the Lord..."

The earthquake shook mountain, crushed rock,
    the wind howled and destroyed,
and Elijah returned to his knowledge
    of the Real Source of All Power.
He feared God again, and Jezebel's puny verbal threat
    was cast in contrast to
    nature's display of God's Sovereign Might.

But the Lord who splits mountains,
who hurls destroying winds,
    was not Elijah's God.

"but the Lord was not in the earthquake"

By his obedience, Elijah was safe from
    the God who cracks the earth.

"And after the earthquake a fire,
but the Lord was not in the fire..."

In the restoration from Jezebel-destruction,
the prophet had to be reminded of the
victory on Mt. Carmel.
The God who IS Fire and sets aflame.

Fire and Flame, this is who God is to the idolater,
One to fear, before whom to tremble.
But for Elijah, this God who is Terror to the Rebellious
came to reassure Elijah He was
not in anger with him.

Elijah had retreated back into the cave in the
face of nature's violence,
shaken by the power of the Lord's display.
Wouldn't you?

But there came to him, in that dark shelter,
"a delicate whispering voice."

*"So it was when Elijah heard it, that
he wrapped his face in his mantle and
went out and stood in the entrance of the cave."*

Throwing his cloak over his face in the surrender
now of healthy fear, he went to the entrance of his cave
to face the One, the Only God.
There he was privy to the gentle whisper of
the God who was, to Elijah… an Understanding Father.

By the precious return of the Fear of God,
    Elijah was restored to his faith and knowledge
        of the True God-of-the-Firey-Sacrifice he
            had known in the past on Mt. Carmel.

And by that godly awe,
he could return to hearing Him,
and cease to hear Jezebel.

The Lord had to return Elijah to faith in
the Terrible Power of His Throne,
        yet at the same time
restore the intimate relationship with a
        Tender Father.

    The storms were for Almighty's enemy;
        the whisper for His servant.

The God of the earthquake and wind was not Elijah's God.
    Elijah, by obedience, knew the gentle ministration
        of a Divine Father who subdued His power to a whisper
        that the frail humanity of the prophet could bear.

Silent faith in God as God
        is more powerful than storm and wind.
Elijah was accustomed to spectacular power displays.
He didn't comprehend the greater power of silence...
        God's quiet and sure confidence in Himself
            marked the eternal end to Jezebel.

God's great understanding of human limitation and frailty
allowed the prophet to confess his unbelief,
    and gently showed him that
        though God was hiding,
           He was not weak, nor was He beaten.

Again the piercing question, sent the second time:
        "What are you doing here, Elijah?"

"What are you doing in this place-of-unbelief?
Come out of it and
    confess your grievance to your Loving Father.
        Talk to Me.
Keep bringing your whining thoughts to Me,
    and in My time, in My own way, I will satisfy you."

Elijah's answer was the same.
He had yet to understand the magnitude of
        what he had just witnessed
        and its meaning to his future.

The Father would have to explain.
    And that was His joy.

Anointing For Judgment

Elijah was assigned to anoint God's choices,
and this was itself a new anointing for Elijah.

To commission kings and prophets is
to rule the future and live in
a transcendent dimension.

"Go, return on your way to the Wilderness of Damascus... "

Damascus was far north from the Sinai of Egypt,
several hundred miles.
To get there Elijah would have to pass through
Jezebel's domain and the valley of her palace.

You can never escape facing Jezebel.
At some point, you will have to
be obedient in the very scene of her treachery.
Go back to the place, the very place where
you left God in fear of that principality –
and walk through, wearing His anointed commission
and by obedience to it, protected.

**To conquer your fear of her is to
dismantle Jezebel-power.**

Face her you will, but by the Lord's enduement of daring;
not anything of human courage.

"… and when you arrive,
anoint Hazael as king over Syria."

Damascus was in Syria, enemy of Israel.
When you are the sworn enemy of
the True God,
by befriending Jezebel,
He will send an enemy against *you*.

Hazael, the instrument of God's chastening,
would bring a reign of terror to Israel that
surpassed Jezebel.

Hazael would burn the fortresses of Israel,
put young men to the sword,
murder children, and rip open the pregnant women.
2 Kings 8:12

And Hazael would continue that destruction
through three successions of Israelite kings.
Even by the son of Hazael would Israel
be chastened for the evil of
Ahab and Jezebel.
2 Kings 13

You must understand that to tolerate Jezebel –
inside of *you* or in the arena of your life –
is to bring against yourself the judgment
of God's Intolerance of her.

The fiery judgment of God is permanently assigned to Jezebel.
She represents a lawlessness, a defiance
so arrogant that she views herself
too powerful even for the God of All.

Should you side with this satanic force,
even by the failure to object,
you will, as Israel
(even under New Testament terms of grace),
be subject to the wrath of God against the disobedient.

*"I will cast her into a sickbed and
those who commit adultery with her
into great tribulation,
unless they repent of their deeds.
I will kill her children with death and
all the churches shall know that
I am He who searches the minds and hearts.
And I will give to each one of you according to your works."*
Revelation 2:22,23

In the end it isn't Jezebel with whom we will deal.
In the final disposition, it will be God Almighty
"with whom we have to do."
He will not condone the Jezebel-evil in *anyone*.
And He will be a terror greater to mankind
than Jezebel could ever hope to be.

He is God.

Seven Thousand

Though cruelty reigns and tyranny
    tries to kill God…
When evil stomps through a land
    and buries its opposition,
God has His secret pockets
    where He hides the pure.

In His time, when He is satisfied, God will answer
    all your dilemmas of life.
God's business first. Then He explains.
As almost an aside to Elijah, an
    "Oh-by-the-way," God said,
"You are not the only one as you suppose."

"Yet I reserve seven thousand in Israel –
all whose knees have not bowed down to Baal… "
1 Kings 19:18

For this age – and these times – God is
largely hidden, His best tales not told,
His faithful children hidden away,
    like some treasure kept out of the sun-glare
    for His enjoyment alone.

Unspoiled because unknown.

Seven, the number of God's rest in His own
    completion and satisfaction.
Thousand, the number of God's order and
    His plenty.

In the midst of Jezebel's mad despotism,
    God dwells in His peaceful satisfaction
        over His unwavering children,
    and His tender care to protect them.

The Amplified Bible translates it this way:
    "I will leave <u>Myself</u> 7000, all…
    the knees that have not bowed to Baal."
    (emphasis mine)

God's gaze is on our worship, our secret bow.
    He marks us by our surrender
        and sequesters those careful of their allegiance.

True devotion is private, entirely.

Who knows the heart? Only God.
Those who fight the pressure of the flesh's god,
    who resist the wave of the current trend,
        who turn their hearts to God,
        meet His special notice.
And He saves them from the evil they resist…
    for Himself, for His private pleasure,
    His rare satisfaction with humanity.

Elijah, fighting his lonely duel with evil,
    knew only his own embattlement;
    his own seeming defeat.

Evil is an always private battle, fought in
    the solitary soul.

You confront tyranny as though it is only,
    only you. No one can help because
      it is not a fight against evil,
      but a personal issue of... ***worship!***

The altar of the **heart** is entirely secret and
    formed in a place only God can witness.
    That temple of the heart is
        the battleground between Jezebel
        and God.
        You choose the winner.
        You build the altar.
        And this is how you win
        and find God's sanctuary.

The war is not "who will imprison you,"
    nor even "who will kill you."
    The battle is not for life, it is for
      the dominion of the soul.
The battle: who will be *your* God?
    And you – alone – form the outcome
      by the bowed knee of
        secret submission.

The battle is not outside...
but entirely *inside*.

God – all along – was enjoying His secret victory
in those who bent the knee of their acquiescence
only to Him and stiffened their stand
against Baal.

And they were hidden from the sword of Jezebel.
Hidden as well from the public prophet,
numbered and counted by a specific regard
of the God for whom Jezebel was simply
a passing point in history, an example allowed
to expose itself for the instruction of the
seven thousand faithful.

This is true in every age and every stage of
God's story in history.

God always moves in secret.
He needs no publicity – delights to move undercover.
His greatest stories will not be known till heaven.
His truest servants will be protected in their worship
and kept pure against the
evil they are willing to fight.
And they will be preserved... for Him...
in seclusion.

Never view God as inactive,
        as unmoving against evil.
        Elijah made that mistake and it
           put him in false despair of self pity,
           and worse, the fallacy of self righteousness.

Almighty has His people,
        and He has His plan.

Wrong is on the throne only temporarily.
        Only by appearance, and not in reality...
        Always!

God will have the last word
        and the ultimate triumph.
        His victory is – at all times – working in secret.
        Always!

The Kiss

"Yet I reserve seven thousand in Israel –
all whose mouths have not kissed him [Baal]"
1 Kings 19:18

Jezebel is Satan's instrument of false romance.
Wherever she invades, there is a flirtation,
> a covert infatuation.

This Hating Enemy cannot bear a "romance with God,"
> so he seeks to steal the Divine Love Affair
> > by allurement into flesh, a tangible lover.

The kiss is the emblem of passion,
> the expression of the heart's secret love.

What you need, you want.
What you want, you love.
> What you love, you kiss.

To love the flesh is to "kiss" Baal.
To need the approval of people is to worship them.
To love the world is to embrace its god
> with a focus and passion that amounts to…
> > a kiss.

The mouth is the place of entrance,
> the door to your being,
the receptivity of what you desire.
To what you value, to that you open your door
> and receive within… *by a kiss.*

Life is sustained through the mouth
and what you love is received through the mouth.

The mouth is the fountain that spews what you are
and the welcome of what you love.

The problem of Jezebel's Baal is
a problem of affection.
The heart's secret lover – *that* you kiss.

Worship is always about love.
You kiss what you love. You do.

It was not only about bowing to this god of flesh-worship.
Jezebel brings romance and that is her mockery
of the God of Love...

To bow is one betrayal, but to love and romance
your idol is ultimate betrayal of the heart.

God is jealous of what you obey *other* than Him.
But He is broken-hearted over what
you love *rather* than Him.

Faith Is Past

Elijah's Lifelong battle
  and his Last battle was with the Jezebel-spirit.

And when he secured her defeat,
    he soared to heaven in a chariot
    and skipped the door of death that all others
      must pass through.

But notice!
    He did not witness her demise;
    he had no hand in her downfall.
    He was raptured long before her death.

He merely heard the proclamation
    of the future ruin of Ahab's realm
    from the Mouth of God.

And he rested in God's victory
    as fully accomplished.

He never anointed Jehu as king.
That was a task inherited by Elisha.

When God declares a thing and just one
of his "listeners" is capable of catching His Voice,
      that word is as good as done,
      and actually constitutes what is *past!*

God does "call those things that are not as
though they are."
And when He names it, it *is.*

The defeat of Jezebel is not a matter of
fight and struggle.

In that ring, you will lose.
Elijah tried wrestling and was crushed.

The demise of Jezebel is entirely
a matter of faith that comes
from hearing, and
hearing straight from God
by waiting in His presence.
Knowing His Voice alone is the victory
and… the *entire victory!*

God's still and sure confidence in Himself
marks the eternal end to Jezebel.

Jezebel Destroys

"[s]eat Naboth in a prominent place among the people. But
seat two scoundrels opposite him and have them testify that
he has cursed both God and the king. Then take him out
and stone him to death."

1 Kings 21:9,10

Never forget, Jezebel destroys.
>With her master, Satan, she
>>aims to destroy God's people
>>totally to the final end of death.

But mere death is not sufficient.
>The malicious appetite for destruction
>>gathers all into its web.

First Jezebel destroys reputations.
>This is the first stroke of her evil genius.
You will always find the whispers
>of insidious lies floating around Jezebel.

And she dupes others into being the
>vessels of her accusation
>>so that her crime is a shared performance.

Jezebel exerts such voracious control
>that you swallow your own identity by
>>the loss of your "no," and
>when that happens, Jezebel can
>>destroy your family,

overthrow the church,
and rule your nation.

Jezebel's insatiable ambition
scrambles your brain
and makes confusion drive your thoughts.

Her control enters your inner being by
the power of witchcraft spewing from rebellion.

By oppressive force, this principality drains the
very energy from your body
and quenches the fire of your soul.
These precious life forces she stole...
even from the zealous Elijah.

So Jezebel captures... the mind, the body, and the soul.
Her intention is to kill your spirit as well.

The ultimate destruction of Jezebel is
the shredding of your relationship with God
by claiming to speak for Him... *as Him.*
So you cannot hear His Personal Voice
for the incessant aggression of
Jezebel's hellish – but religious – logic.

By fierce control of your choices, your time,
your peace,
she quenches the Spirit in your life
and takes His sacred place...

When someone takes over God's place in your life,
  behind that control is the
    Jezebel spirit of Satan.

And you lose God by the violent seizure of His throne
  in the mind of your heart...
    by the cold grip of fear.

Jezebel demands to be the only relationship you have
  by disregarding any other ties,
    no matter how legitimate.

  Especially does she seize your
    relationship with God
    and consumes it as her own...

Elijah Restores

"And [Jesus'] disciples asked Him, saying
'Why then do the scribes say that Elijah must come first?'"

"Jesus answered and said to them,
'Indeed, Elijah is coming first and will restore all things.'"
Matthew 17:10,11

The terrible motivation of Jezebel is Satan's own
    savage hatred for God.
    And that is the real goal –
    to get at God through those He saves…
        and loves.

    To beat Him! To humiliate God!
    To kill His plans and His sheep.
    All to get at Him.
    This is Jezebel by Satan's insane rage
        toward the One Who Rules.

You and I are simply the pawns of
    Satan's Game of Hatred,
    played against God because He is God.
    And because He loves us…

So Jezebel disturbs the relationship with God
    by her loud interference.
    When she can separate the believer
        from this Good Father by the
        means of her intimidation and lies,
            she has secured her destruction.

Then the Father sends the Holy Spirit in the Elijah mantle
and begins to woo back to Himself
the widow: the woman in frightened control,
and the boy: the man in sick weakness.

When Elijah had fully demonstrated God's goodness
to those wrecked lives under Satan's dominion,
and they were restored to a
Miracle Giving Father,
his role was accomplished.

So in the end times, Elijahs sent from God
will restore the essential connection
to God by the knowledge of Him
as a Precious Father.
And also to the Glorious Son.

The church is to be built on this rock:
the revelation of who Jesus is –
the Exalted Son of God.

And this recognition comes,
as it did for Simon Peter,
by the living experience of
exposure to the Trinity.
Personal – private – individual…
relationship is the key.

Relationship.
That's what God restores by the Elijah-spirit.

The foundation of persons, of families, and nations is
relationship with God.

Without communion with God as
the primary bedrock of the individual,
society collapses –
all the way from the smallest soul
to the governing power of an entire nation…

This was the state of Elijah's Israel.
Jezebel had not merely seized the throne of government,
"she" had dared to take over God's throne.

Or so it seemed…

God's throne has never been challenged.
His rule has never – ever – been shaken.
Behind all the ruin of humanity and the evil of Satan,
God's throne is utterly intact
and He reigns in Perfect Calmness…
always.

Any usurper of His Dominion can only be temporary.
He will rise to defend His throne over your life
and the ultimate right to His cherished child.

Elijah was sent first to restore
one oppressed widow and one perishing boy
to relationship with a Caring Father.

Knowing God is *individual* long before it is corporate.

From that small beginning,
   from the ministry to a singular person,
   Elijah was launched on a journey
   to Full Restoration of the entire nation
      from the ruin of Jezebel.

Elijah himself experienced the loss of his intimacy with God
      and was driven from The Father's Safe Wing
      by the paralyzing lie of Jezebel's power.

Whenever you live under that lie,
you dwell in the Desert of Fear,
      which is really the Wilderness of Unbelief.
      There you lose connection with
      the power of God's Sovereignty
      and the goodness of Father's heart.

The first restoration is to the fear of God.

   Terror and blindness – that is fear of Satan.
   Reverence and recognition – that is the fear of God.

Elijah's own reverence for God was restored by
      the earth shakings of Mount Sinai/Horeb.
   Only at the end of that heaving did
      the Tender Voice come to him.

You have to experience Elijah's personal trek
      to bear an Elijah mantle in the
         Last Days.

This strange prophet was called "Elijah" by Jesus Himself.
John the Baptist came in his wild raiment
>with a shouting message of drastic holiness.
>>And he brought back
>>>such a respect for God,
>>>such a vision of His Majesty,
>>>that people repented *en masse.*

By that return to the recognition of God,
>through a gripping repentance,
>>the Father was restored to their hearts.
>>And they were made receptive to the
>>>Coming Son.

Elijah-of-the-Last-Days will meet the final mad attempt
>of Jezebel to seize the vulnerable sheep
>>before the Return of Christ.

Through your own relationship with God,
>sustained *by HIM,* seasoned by experience,
>the Elijah-anointing will level the
>>mountains of ubiquitous pride,
>>bring up the valleys of the tyrannized-broken –
>>one last time –
>and prepare God's people,
>through breaking their Jezebel chain,
>>to welcome the Conquering Jesus.
>>>The True Monarch.

The restoration of God as Father on
   the Throne of your soul's intimacy is
   "the restoration of all things" [1]
   since **in** God, you possess His "all things." [2]

The gift of the Trinity, by the Father, Son, and Holy Spirit,
   is the entire health and peace of the mind.
   The restoration of physical strength and
   the zeal of the Lord of Hosts.

What Jezebel has killed by generations of oppression
   is restored to overflowing fullness
      by the bestowing of the Spirit.

But notice please. **The restoration comes by Elijah!**
   By the welcoming the prophet,
   to the return of the prophetic office.

[1] Matthew 17:11
[2] 1 Cor. 3:22

Ahab Must Die

Jezebel and Ahab are a marriage of the demonic.
A partnership of hell.

Satan especially relishes imposing this twosome
into a Christian marriage for the defeat of both
husband… and wife.

This "liaison" creeps also into the Church, into
the brother and sister kinship,
producing a sick alliance,
and counterfeiting true unity of the Spirit.

Jezebels create Ahabs and
Ahabs call for Jezebels.
Where one is, the other is also there, entangled
in a mutual need-and-hate alliance
built on the fear of both.

And if Jezebel sets you up to be her Ahab and
you should garner the courage to refuse,
her violent rage will blast you with
vicious and ongoing "divorce."

Ahab would give you control,
choose you to receive his burden of blame,
and bear his load of responsibility.
If you dare to reject the job,

his self pity will pound you and his whine torture you
with the condemnation that you are a failure.
Completely.
Especially a *spiritual* failure.

Ahab and Jezebel fit by a harmony of evil dependence,
and they need each other in order to "be."
Jezebel requires someone to rule over
and Ahab must have someone to blame.

Both spirits can also live and function in one person,
in a horror of contradiction.

The next phase of Jezebel's defeat was
the breakup of the evil-marriage by the death of Ahab.
The weakness of cowardice and fear must be killed.
Jezebel-rule is over when Ahab-fear is annihilated.
"If your right hand offends you cut it off."

The liaison was dissolved by death.
The king who kept her power intact
by his weak subjection, died a coward
in a battle he was loathe to fight.

Elijah had no fear of the sissy, Ahab.
When you will not fight, then everyone can rule you.
This is why Ahab would do all Elijah said.
Even his enemy could turn him.

This is the story of Ahab's death:
Ben-Hadad, king of Syria, sent to Ahab this message:
*"Your silver and your gold are mine,
your loveliest wives and children are mine."*

And Ahab, unwilling to fight for his family,
without even a single protest, answered,
"I and all I have are yours."

"Anything but fight." This is the Ahab-spirit.
Never confront. "Yes" to any degree of tyranny.

Such an easy win for the Syrian king, he would go for more.
The Ahab-appeasing of your enemy only increases his appetite…
and his audacity.

*"I will send my servants to you tomorrow
about this time, and they shall search your house
and the houses of your servants.
And it shall be that whatever is pleasant in your eyes,
they will put in their hands and take it."*
1 Kings 20:6

The nature of Ahab is ultimate laziness and self saving.
He would comply with the loss and suffering of others,
even his family, just to keep from fighting!
Any compromise, any sacrifice so he could save himself.
Ahab is "peace at any price."
Only when it was an invasion into his very house and favorite
treasures did he begin to object and seek help.

Only now did the king of Israel reported
    to the elders and people.
    By their outrage, and the prophet's promise of
      victory, Ahab finally went to war.
God, defending His own name, effected the victory.

But in the end, Ahab made an unnecessary
    treaty with the enemy.
That's Ahab. Always contracting with the enemy.
    First, he sold himself to do evil by Jezebel's enticing.
    Then he made a foolish bargain with a
      king under God's angry judgment.
    And that treaty was made so he could be
      in the marketplace.
    Once again, for personal gain, he cavorted with evil.
                1 Kings 20:34

Three years later, Syria came again to war against Israel
and Ahab enticed Jehoshaphat, king of Judah, to join his war.

Jehoshaphat was a good king, but bore a
    fatal Ahab-like weakness;
    a false goodness, that would – but for prayer –
    be his undoing.

Ahab planned the battle and decided Jehoshaphat would
    wear his kingly garb.
Thinking to hide behind Jehoshaphat's conspicuous presence,
Ahab went to battle disguised as an ordinary soldier,
pretending not to be the King God had made him.

He schemed to escape danger
    by putting another in the forefront.
    This is always the way of an Ahab:
    hiding from responsibility, saving himself and
        throwing others in the path of his own danger.

Jehoshaphat, mistaken for Ahab, was surrounded by Syrian
chariots but he cried out to God and the enemies saw he was
not the king of Israel. So they left him to return safely to his
own throne.

Ahab, who intended Judah's king to die in his stead,
was shot by a random arrow of God's inescapable judgment
        and bled to death in his chariot.
    Dogs licked his blood in the very place
    of Naboth's murder by the hand of Ahab-compliance,
        just as Elijah had predicted.
                1 Kings 21:19; 22:38

Weakness and passivity always come full circle
    to find you out in the caves of your cowardice.
Cringing before the fight, holding on to
    selfishness above integrity,
        Ahab stands forever as a compromise with evil.
            Always siding with God's mortal enemy
            simply by avoiding the struggle.
        Saving his skin and sacrificing everyone else's.
            This is Ahab.

He died before Jezebel died.

So too, our cowardice has to die
> before Jezebel can be cast down from the tower of her
> satanic presumption over our lives.

Ahab – in you and in me – must die
> before Jezebel-power is destroyed.

Elijah of the Last Days

When "Elijah" comes again it will be to herald the "great and terrible day of the Lord."

Jehu, Anointed King

God had chosen the next king to succeed Ahab.
By naming that man and calling for his anointing,
God was declaring the Ahab-Jezebel throne
   terminated,
an accomplished fact in the Divine Mind.

Chosen on Mount Horeb long before he knew it,
Jehu was simply a warrior, commander in the army of Israel.
   Elisha sent an unnamed prophet to anoint Jehu
      with the oil of this commission:

> *"Thus says the Lord God of Israel:*
> *'I have anointed you king over Israel.*
> *You shall strike the house of Ahab your master,*
> *that I may avenge the blood of my servants the prophets*
> *and the blood of all the servants of the Lord,*
> *at the hand of Jezebel."*
> *"For the whole house of Ahab shall perish, and I will cut*
> *off from Ahab every male person, both*
> *bond and free in Israel."*
> 2 Kings 9: 6-8 (Emphasis mine)

Ahab-weakness of letting Jezebel rule will not
be allowed to exist in
   God's spiritual kingdom. Not one part. Not in one place.
      Do you understand?

With fantastic zeal, Jehu seized his mission from God;
  mounted a chariot and rode furiously to Jezreel,
    the valley of Jezebel's palace.
Two kings watched his approach with trepidation:
  Joram (king of Israel), son of Ahab and Jezebel,
  and Ahaziah (king of Judah), grandson of
    Ahab and Jezebel.

Twice, horsemen were sent to inquire of Jehu's company:
  "Is it peace?" (Are you coming in peace?)
Twice, Jehu replied, *"What have you to do with peace?"*
  (You know nothing about peace.)

Finally, both kings in their separate chariots went to meet Jehu
  at the field of Naboth, the man Jezebel had murdered
    so Ahab could possess his vineyard.

"King Joram demanded, 'Do you come in peace, Jehu?'
Jehu replied, 'How can there be peace as long as the idolatry
and witchcraft of your mother, Jezebel, are all around us?'"
  2 Kings 9:22 NLT

Both Ahab-descended kings were killed then and there.
Thus began the entire annihilation of the Ahab empire
  according to God's command.

At last, Jezebel's end had come:

"When Jehu came to Jezreel, Jezebel heard of it,
and she painted her eyes and adorned her head
and looked out the window.
As Jehu entered the gate, she said, 'Is it well, Zimri,
your master's murderer?'"
2 Kings 9:30,31

The woman had learned that Jehu's sword had killed
both her son and grandson.

Jehu did not answer Jezebel a word,
nor did he defend himself from her accusation.
He did not speak to her at all!
Such is a king's dealing with Jezebel.

He entered the courtyard of her palace;
utterly immune to her seduction,
and without fear of her intimidation!

This new king merely looked up at her tower window and
asked the everlasting question God asks
when Jezebel is reigning.
"Who is on my side? Who?"

When two or three eunuchs looked down at him,
"[Jehu] said, 'Throw her down.' So they threw her down
and some of her blood was sprinkled on the wall
and on the horses, and he trampled her under foot."
2 Kings 9:32,33

Jehu's chariot finished the breaking of her body;
    symbol that the enemy lies crushed under the King's feet.
Gruesome death by a calm commander,
    who sat down to eat in peace
        at the very place of Jezebel-rule.
While he feasted in victory,
    Jezebel was eaten by dogs who licked
    her blood and left only a few bones to bury.

Jehu brought God's word to utter completion.
    All was fulfilled to the last detail.

Who was this Jehu, tearing through the realm of
    Baal, destroying its worshipers,
        altars, pillars and temple,
    until it is stated *"Jehu destroyed Baal from Israel."*
                      2 Kings 10:28

Who was this Jehu, fearless victor where even
    the bravest faltered?

Who was this Jehu, possessed of such authority
    that he commanded Jezebel's death
    and it was instantly executed?

Who was this Jehu, whose power ruled over the
    last vestige of Ahab-evil and destroyed
    even the friends of his reign?

Jehu stands in "type and shadow" to
    represent the **Lord Jesus Christ.**

Christ: the Real and Ultimate King
    whose victory in the far distant future was
    the hidden meaning of this Old Testament story.

And in the story of Jehu, we see a sure glimpse
    of the "zeal of the Lord of Hosts"...
    a passion so much greater than the force of any evil,
        a fervor that conquers with ease
        what humanity cannot handle!

Only the Son of God could conquer the Father's
    mortal enemy, but His triumph
    was so perfect and complete that
    today nothing is left to Jezebel's power.

"When He [God] had disarmed the rulers and authorities,
He made a public display of them,
having triumphed over them through Him [Christ]."
Colossians 2:15

Even today that Jehu-question rings from the message
    to Thyatira on the other side of the Cross.
    The same ominous query regarding Jezebel tolerance--
        the question demanding a decision
        and an answer--
        asked of you. . . of me. . .

Who is on My side? Who?

Peace was the sole concern of Jezebel-descendants.
The two kings who had learned to condone infamy
and believed peace came from "tolerance of Jezebel."

Peace in Israel came,
    not from compromise with tyranny,
    not from co-existence with evil.
Peace in Israel came
    by separation and violence,
    by confrontation and upheaval
        through the sword of Jehu...

Peace at any price is always the loss of peace.
Peace is not harmony among people.
    Real peace exists only with God.
    Serenity flows from *His* satisfaction,
    and ever *follows* the Sword.

Jesus said it this way,
    "Do not suppose that I have come to bring peace
    to the earth. I did not come to bring peace,
    but a sword. For I have come to turn,
    'a man against his father,
    a daughter against her mother,
    a daughter-in-law against her mother-in-law —
    a man's enemies will be
    the members of his own household.'"
        Matt. 10:34

The Corpse of Jezebel

By the choice to leave Jezebel comes the faith to throw her
   out of the elevated window of her presumption.

Without the choice, there will be no courage...
      therefore no victory.

Decision is our only responsibility. All else follows that!
   Decision toward God shifts the universe of your realm
      into His power and He is free to move as King.
   God limits Himself to the sphere of your private choices.
   So when you turn by the simple act of decision,
   He turns toward you to impart His character into
      your very being
   and His secret power storms in your behalf.

By a gruesome death, nothing was left but her
     "skull, her feet and her hands."
                 2 Kings 9:35

Her "thinking" and "doing" was killed out of Israel.
The evil blood of her life spilled for unclean dogs to drink.

Just as Elijah had said,
       "On the plot of ground at Jezreel, dogs
         shall eat the flesh of Jezebel."
               verse 36

Jezebel was rendered an empty corpse,
    a pile of dung without even a grave to visit.

> *"[a]nd the corpse of Jezebel shall be as refuse*
> *on the surface of the field, in the plot at Jezreel,*
> *so that they shall not say, 'here lies Jezebel.'"*
>
> verse 37 NKJ

Jezebel is the test of our loyalty, the trial of our faith.
But we hold HER life and death *in our hands,*
    and not the reverse!

The Cross Has Won

Jezebel-power was utterly and completely destroyed
    at the bloody cross, as were all the
        disguises of Satan.

*"He [Jesus] too shared in their humanity so that by His
death He might destroy him who holds the power of death —
that is, the devil."*
Heb. 2:14 NIV

Jezebel-by-Satan was
marched through the heavens in the train of
    a Conquering Hero, humiliated by His glory,
    a captured prisoner in His wake.
This principality was
    stripped of authority... of power... of dominion.

And that victory was total down to the last vestige of
        Satan's horrible evil.

All the angels witnessed it.
The company of heaven saw it.
And they must marvel at our blindness to it.

Just as Jehu searched out all the relatives, court
    attendants, sons and friends of Ahab,
    and slew them...
so has the Son of God conquered all... all... all.
    Total Victory, by His
    Complete Dominion.
    Perfect Success.

The pivot of history is the Cross of Jesus Christ!
   Elijah saw it as the certain future and
   such was the glory of that vision that
   Elijah soared to heaven because of it.

What Elijah could not do even with
   his severe obedience,
Jesus, Son of the Most High God,
   would secure by the spilling of His
own Holy Blood, the sure defeat of all evil.

Standing in for all the evil mankind
   embraces *and* is willing to embody,
Jesus was cast down to the ground
and His blood poured on the earth
     by God's judgment of death against
     the sin of humanity and
     the evil of Satan.

We have been liberated from Jezebel.
   We have total victory over any place of
     her vile intrusion.
   We cast her down by the Past Event of
   the Cross, proclaiming her defeat
— not as a future event to be secured by
   intense fighting —
    but an accomplished fact
     by the Zeal of the Lord of Hosts
     Who was willing to die for
   Satan's destruction and our freedom.

We do not now live in a war zone of struggle,
    a wrestling match with evil.

We live in the realm of a Past Conquest.
    We live in the Victory of our King.
    "Now the prince of this world will be driven out."

    John 12:31

But there is still in Christ's Kingdom the
    captured-enemy, pretending he is undefeated,
        strutting by a power that has been –
            in Reality – rendered ineffective.

The territory has been conquered, but
    the enemy perpetrates his lie –
    still the **lie** of Jezebel:
"I have a power that is unconquerable, even by God."

Jezebel is always present where the Church,
    the Body of Christ, is in operation.

Wherever there is religion *about God*
        instead of relationship with *God*,
        there will Jezebel set her throne
        and posture herself to rule rulers
            and weaklings.

Wherever the prophetic office rises to
proclaim the current Voice of God,
        there will Jezebel oppose and kill.

Satan's Jezebel is like a condemned criminal
waiting for the sure execution but who
continues to pose as one with terrifying power.

But it is an outlandish LIE.
Jezebel's harassment and oppression of believers
        is all illegitimate.
"She" has no rights, no ground against God's children.

It is not for us to struggle with that spirit.
That will ensure our humiliating defeat.
To struggle and anguish is to believe in Satan, not God.

It is not for us to "be nice" to the aspects of Jezebel.
That is betrayal of our Lord who paid so dearly
        for "her" destruction.

Our victory lies in this: to believe that Jesus
        has cast Jezebel-Satan down to utter death.
To hold to that faith as accomplished fact.
No matter what happens or what evil work appears,
to declare it, to speak it, and to command it.

Our victory lies in faith-like-Elijah, who
saw it in the future and rested in its certainty.
We must "see" it in the Divine Past and
        rest in Christ's victory in the
        secret place of our heart.

By an Event in History, already accomplished,
        Jezebel has been thrown down.

If you *believe* in wrestling with Jezebel, you shall wrestle!
If you *believe* in a long term struggle with the Jezebel-spirit,
that will be precisely your experience.

But if you will work toward this:
to "**believe** in the Son whom God has sent" (John 6:28)
and that His death earned a legal defeat for the
Satanic disguise of Jezebel,
then you will see the end of Jezebel's power
over *you*.

"She" might remain as a presence, but there will
be no power or threat she can exert over you.
You will stand in complete safety wrapped inside the
very Life of Jesus Christ.

According to His final prayer with you in mind,
you will be kept "from the evil one"
untouchable,
immovable
and fully immune.

Rejoice Church! Jezebel has been thrown down!
Jezebel is defeated!

Elijah of the Last Days

The prophecy of John the Baptist,
  spoken by Isaiah was this:

> *"The voice of one crying in the wilderness,*
> *Prepare the way of the Lord,*
> *Make His paths straight.*
> *Every valley shall be filled and every mountain*
> *and hill brought low.*
> *The crooked places shall be made straight,*
> *And the rough ways smooth and all flesh shall see*
> *the salvation of God."*
>
> Luke 3:5,6 NKJ

Elijah revealed the Zeal of the Lord and
  exposed His Holy Opposition to Jezebel.

Elijah was covered with and empowered by the Spirit of God.

To welcome the Lord of Glory to this dirty world,
  there was and will be, always Elijah clearing the way,
  leveling the mountains of arrogance
  and bringing up the valleys of despair.

The Spirit of God in His Elijah-character
  dwelled in two individuals.

Elijah of the Old Testament and
John the Baptist of the New.

In the Last Days
of Jezebel's final fury,
the Spirit of Christ will again come as
Elijah to straighten the path for
the Second Glorious Return.

There will be a great difference in this Elijah, however.
He will not dwell only in an individual, one here and one there.
I believe the Spirit of God will pour the Elijah spirit
on the Entire Church by an *inward indwelling*
that neither Elijah nor John knew.

The Church, being those who nestle under
absolute dominion of their Lord... Jesus.

The Church as a Vast Body of His Headship will
embody "Elijah" and rise as a corporate unit
filled with zeal for the Bride of Jesus to be
cleansed from the filth of Jezebel and
liberated from "her" oppression.

Elijah of the Last Days will, for the first time,
be a corporate-Elijah.
And in that unity of purpose,
that enormous Fervor of the Holy Spirit,
this Church will cast down Jezebel to a certain death
by the power and unction of a Bloody Savior.

John was beheaded by the Jezebel-spirit for his exposure
of Satan's religious presence.

This time, as Elijah appears again out of an obscure past
for his part on the stage of God's Final Triumph,
the head of Jezebel – the diabolical Satanic thinking –
will be cast down from its arrogant tower
as an empty skull.

(2 Kings 9:35, 2 Cor. 10:4-6)

The extraordinary revelation of God in Elijah will spread
throughout the Living Body of Christ and
Jezebel will be exposed as never before.

Jezebel will be unveiled and known
by her vile name wherever "she-in-Satan"
constructs her throne and murders God's prophets.

Thrown down by the suffering eunuchs of her tyranny,
Jezebel will be swept out of the path of the
Returning Saviour-King,
not this time on the back of a common donkey
but in the Clouds of His Glory coming to gather
His Bride, victorious and shining,
pure in character,
and free of Jezebel!

Robed in Spotless Purity, she – the Church –
will have gained,
by a simple faith in His Victory over evil!

Overcomers

Jezebel is merely a test…
sent to burn Jezebel
out of you and me.

Overcomers' Reward

Jesus Himself, speaking about Jezebel in Revelation 2,
 promised great reward to those who cast her down...

"And he who overcomes (is victorious) and
who obeys My commands to the (very) end
(doing the works that please me)
I will give him authority and power over the nations;
and he shall rule them with a scepter (rod) of iron, as when
earthen pots are broken in pieces, and (his power over
them shall be) that which I Myself have received
from My Father."

Rev. 2 Amplified Bible

Our trials at the hands of Jezebel have a Divine Purpose
 that overrides all the plans of God's enemy.

If God permits you to be sifted by Jezebel it is for
  the formation of
  His Glorious Idea of you.

All humanity is weak and sniveling.
  Cowards we are, by inherited nature.

Jezebel has the intention to ride that human fear
  to her overpowering dominion.
God has His intention as well... to consume our terror
    with **fire**.
  The blaze He often uses is... Jezebel.

Jezebel will run you, threaten you, destroy you,
  until by the ruin of all, you no longer
    are afraid of what she can do,
      even to the loss of your literal life.
                                        Rev. 12:11

There is a strength of spirit – a steel fearlessness –
  that God wants to form in us.

        It is not a strength of humanness.
          That would be mere flesh.

        Rather, the power of a pure spirit
            that knows God by an Elijah-intimacy,
          a lonely and solitary believer –
            stripped of desire for the world's allurement
          through relentless suffering at the hands of
            Jezebel-crushing.

Jezebel – in the end – is the preparation of the Bride
          for her Throne and Scepter.

Jezebel provokes human fear,
    but this only serves to expose it
      in all its self-saving methods.

        "Their weakness was turned to strength."
                              Heb. 11

How? By suffering…
By the fire of God burning out of YOU and ME,
   the stone altars we built to save our own skin
      and indulge our flesh.
  A burning fire until all that is left is
  a pure-Elijah-character molded by the Holy Spirit
   into a transformed-likeness to the
      Immovable Rock, Jesus Christ.

Weakness changed into divine strength and
           fear transformed into steadfast faith:
this is the overcoming and its reward is a Throne of Steel
  and Scepter of Authority, reigning with Christ forever.

By His Impeccable Sovereignty brooding over all,
  the Father uses the queen of Satan,
   to purify the Bride of His Lovely Son.

So the dreadful fight has a vast reward.
  Through the dark passage of Jezebel-cruelty,
   there is a Waiting Entrance to Eternal Glory.
     Worth it all!!

Eunuchs And Weaklings

"Now when Jehu had come to Jezreel,
Jezebel heard of it: and
she put paint on her eyes and adorned her head
and looked through a window.
Then as Jehu entered at the gate, she said,
'Is it peace, Zimri, murderer of your master?'"
2 Kings 9:30,31 NKJ

Deluded by confidence in her lewd power to seduce,
    Jezebel thought to fascinate Jehu
  even while falsely accusing him of
      that which was her own sin – murder.
    Brazen woman with clouded mirror;
      hideously ugly, and not seeing it.

Jehu, aloof by his anointed authority as king over her,
      didn't bother to answer.
Her self confidence was a delusion,
    Jehu's compelling calm was a divine reality.

Instead of answering, he called out for volunteers and
    the eunuchs peered
    out from her window.

Eunuchs, those men castrated, ruined by Jezebel.
Their masculine seed destroyed under her despotic control.

Spiritually translated, "eunuchs" represent those whose
    fruitfulness, passion, and energy have been
    crushed and buried in some grave of the soul,
    living half a life, humanly alive but dead in gender.
    Men and women, both – eunuchs of gender-futility
    by Jezebel-cruelty.

We the weaklings, given the call, have complete
    authority by the Word of the King,
    to throw down Jezebel-in-Satan
    from any towering stronghold where
      her presence rules and seduces,
      on any hill of our world.

King Jehu-as-Jesus did not himself touch her.
    He offered that right to her victims…
      as King with authority,
      as One higher than her presumed position,
        He simply called the mutilated victims
        of Jezebel butchery
      to use their superior position
      under the Real King.

We are commanded to defeat her. Even as the weakest, most
trembling victim of her oppression, we still have that
    Winning Authority behind us as God's children.

He who is "in us is greater" than
    the Jezebels loose in the world.

Jehu called first for a choice.

"And he [Jehu] looked up at the window and said,
"Who is on my side? Who?"
So two or three eunuchs looked out at him."
2 Kings 9:32 NKJ

Significant choice! Jezebel-by-Satan traps you to her control
    by the force of a LIE that you cannot escape,
  that you are bound and forever caught under her power.
  But the right to choose is intact. And choice is enough.
    We can choose God… always, always.

Sacred choice!
    The decision away from Jezebel and toward God, is
      the beginning of "her" end.
The prison is easily left by the simple decision to
  be on *God's side.*

Jezebel forces the consummate choice,
    "To whom will you CHOOSE to belong?"

Before the universe, YOU have the right of choice.
    Who is on God's side?
Jezebel may capture you, destroy your fruitfulness,
    drag you to the tower of her evil.
But when the King of Kings calls, your choice alone
    will determine your escape.

If you choose God, then you may throw Jezebel down to
    her own crushing death over your life –
      over any arena, any person –
      where she presumes control.

"Then he said, 'throw her down.'"
verse 33

In an ironic turn, Jehu gave the privilege of her demise
into the hands of her weak victims.

This Eternal Permission belongs to us, and is given by
the Savior whose Holy Blood is
the dread and terror of Satan.
Behind His command to "throw her down" is
Everlasting Authority over Satan, earned at great cost.
And by this authority of the King, we command.

It is ours to do! Do you understand? The privilege of
defeating her is a *responsibility* to do so;
a call to every believer by
a New Testament summons
to oppose the ancient Jezebel-tyranny.
We must see the Burning Judgment of God
against *condoning* that evil,
stated in the letter to the church at
Thyatira...

"I will kill her [Jezebel's] children with death,
and all the churches shall know that I am He
who searches the minds and hearts."
Rev. 2:23

Jezebel is the disguise of Satan, the one who is
the mortal enemy of God and
murderer of His children.

To allow her rule is to choose hell for yourself
    but the real consequence is the
        loss of God's protective favor…
        by deliberate choice.

Beyond even that, we must see God's fiery opposition
    and absolute hatred for the Jezebel principality.
His Pure Indignation is even toward His own children,
        those who – by perverted loyalty –
        let His mortal enemy be their master.

The Suffering King rules Jezebel.
It is only for His subjects to believe…

Two Currents of Humanity

There are two deadly currents of all humanity.
We are either
    compliant… the Ahab tendency
    or controlling… Jezebel propensity.

In these excesses of Ahab and Jezebel, God
has revealed our human frailty…
    the strong and the weak.

For some, really for most of us, both flaws
    – the weakness of will and the dominance of selfishness –
can be present in one person.

Human tendencies, fruit of original sin:
Adam-compliance and Eve-overpowering –
    humanity's ripeness for satanic invasion.

    That inherited sin-nature is so ingrained that
    there is no changing it, no altering the tendencies.

The only remedy for it was their grave:
    Ahab-cowardice must die. Jezebel-control must perish.
        The burial of that sin-person is a past fact.
    But the freedom from it is found in a
        process of experience.

You are already dead but you must come *into* the death.
    Divine Mystery of solution.

Many follow God who do not die.
Many serve Him who will not perish.

Jezebel and Ahab are consummate pictures of
   self-preservation;
survivors using illegitimate means to play god to their world.
   Ahab complying to keep Jezebel calm.
   Jezebel ruling to keep Ahab compliant.

God does not call us to conquer Jezebel/Ahab
   with a fight.
He calls us to **die** by daily surrender to Him
   and refusal of any other ruler,
      even the tyrant of "self."

Only the cross defeats God's enemy.
   The Cross of Jesus Christ has achieved
      the legal end of Satan.

My internal cross is experienced through obedience
   (and ONLY through obedience),
   private and individual, known by knowing God's Son.
   And resolutely going His direction.

Only obedience frees me from the Jezebel-Ahab conspiracy.
   And obedience brings me to the end of
      that conspiracy within ME.

My cross takes me into the grave I entered
      long ago… with Him… but more wonderful, into
      the resurrection I share IN Him.

One Life, and only One Life, did not succumb to
    the sin nature of weakness and tyranny.

Only One. Jesus dwelled in humanity but lived by God;
    in the perfect balance of pure
    acquiescence and rightful dominion.

His Resurrected Life, His glorious purity
    is given — not to "cover" us but
to indwell us, to be our personal purity
    by the very nature of God.

His life alone knows
        when to yield and when to resist.
        When to be silent and when to speak,
        when to lead and when to follow.
        When to turn over the money tables…

His life alone is in perfect harmony with God.
    And that Amazing Life is mine.

To possess it I must die out of my body,
become an empty earthen vessel for the
        Surpassing Glory of the Son of God.

*"If we have been united with him like this in his death,
    we will certainly also be united with him
        in his resurrection."*
Romans 6:5

Elijah's chariot is a picture of the finale of
   a life of obedience and communion with the Father.
      A glorious end,
      destination Heaven, in a
   miraculous transcendence over death.

This death-by-transcendence is pictured in Elijah who
   perished from earth without a literal death.
Soar into heaven he escaped by a resurrection chariot.

   God would have you soar above the common
      human cowardice and tyranny.

Death is the solution to Jezebel and Ahab.
      Mine. Yours.
Death is God's remedy to the ruin of humanity by
      the greed of Eden.

Real victory over Jezebel-Ahab is not
   the death of that "other" person, but MY OWN.

Their death is a picture of those
   sin tendencies in ME
   that must be pierced with the arrow of God's Speaking
   and cast down from the tower of natural arrogance
      to total death.

But resurrection is the goal, the result of obedient death.
   Not future, but in this life.
      In the Now of Christ. The Resurrected Jesus.

Seated far above principalities and powers,
reigning over Jezebels and Ahabs.
When we can leave this world by the chariot of obedience,
and see our real position, seated with Him
in the very Heavenlies,
we will find those vile enemies under our feet
because of the Living Son in whom
God is well pleased.

*"Since then you have been raised with Christ, set your
hearts on things above, where Christ is seated at the
right hand of God.*

*"For you died, and your life is now hidden
with Christ in God.*

*"Put to death therefore, whatever belongs
to your earthly nature..."*
Colossians 3:1,3,5

Love and Hate

The universe is not about right versus wrong,
   nor even good and evil.

The meaning of the universe,
   the purpose of the whole creation,
      is *Love.*
      And the assault of its opposition: Hate.

Love and hate are not feelings. Not philosophies.
Love and hate
   are two spiritual beings in the universe.
      They are actually God, Who is LOVE;
         and Satan, who is Hate.

Hate came into Eden and suggested that LOVE did not love.
   And those pure two who lived within the caress of LOVE,
      began to lose – through Hate – LOVE's covering.
      And they were made naked and ashamed.

      They entered Hate by
      receiving its thoughts
      of contempt for LOVE.

Now the lowly clay is born knowing how to Hate the Potter,
   just because He is the Potter.
   From childhood wounds, by adult disappointments,
      bitterness with God festers and multiplies
      by streams of Hate's unforgiving thoughts until
         the flood rises and the soul is
         drowned under hatred of God…

Then amazingly, the hate-filled-person rises
    to "serve" Him he hates!
"Those who hate the Lord would pretend obedience to Him."
                       Psalm 81:15

The person who becomes entangled with Jezebel-evil
    is a person who harbors in secret…
        an underlying and excessive hatred for God.
    And … the motive to murder Him.

Jezebel-captives are God-haters who want to control
    what God failed to manage,
    to pay back what He would not avenge.
        And whose fury at the world is sure evidence
        of rage with God for personal wrongs and pains.

Sinners did not kill God on the cross.
It was the religious sons of hell,
        the God-haters, who devised it.
    Liars who forgot they hate God.
    Imposters who kill Him while hailing His name.

Whether the religion is atheism or Christianity,
    or all in between,
    jezebel-servers run as religious zealots
    to the places where they can best get at God,
        to wreck and ravage His sheep.
    And that is usually right in the middle of
        the church.

The prime target of Jezebel-killers are the
    succulent lambs who love LOVE. . .

What About You?

Are you the **vessel** of Jezebel? or Ahab?

What if you come to the see in utter shock that you
      have lived and survived either by
      Jezebel-domination or Ahab-weakness?
    That you have used and welcomed this
      until you have been taken over by it?

To *see* that you are — caught in the
      system of Jezebel is a miracle in itself.
    Part of the scheme is to keep you blinded to
      the unseen force of Satan's presence.

THE ROOT
      of Jezebel/Ahab captivity is a
        buried hatred of God.

Jezebel controls to have her/his way.
Ahab surrenders to have his/her way.
Both excesses are to gain control.

The control is rebellion that comes from unbelief.
The belief is: God will not protect me or supply me
      because *God is not good.*
    I must be good to myself.
The control is: God is not powerful or interested in me
      because *God is not really on the throne.*
    I must take charge myself.

The problem is not childhood abuses, nor wounds of a spouse.
It is not an alcoholic parent, nor a religious father.
    It is none of these...

        The problem is not what *happened* to you.
        The problem is *you!*

Sin is failure to love God;
but evil is outright hatred for Him.

All humanity fails in loving the Creator,
        but hatred of life's trouble
        becomes malice toward Him.

> *"See that no one comes short of the grace*
> *of God, that no root of bitterness springing up*
> *causes trouble and by it many are defiled..."*
>   Hebrews 12:15

THE BRANCH
        of Jezebel-evil finds its home in bitterness,
        in a soul, sick with old and rotting lists
        of unforgiven wrongs.

Unforgiveness is a stage on which the devil can rehearse
        the scenes of your injustice and you sit
        in the audience, reviewing the pictures and words,
            remembering, remembering...
                over and over and over and...

Bitterness is hurt cherished past sundown.
It becomes the nest devils dig
in your soul
to infect your whole being
with Satan's very own rage toward God.

"When angry, do not sin; do not ever let your wrath
(your exasperation, your fury or indignation)
last until the sun goes down.
Leave no [such] room or foothold for the devil
[give no opportunity to him]."
Ephesians 4:26, 27 Amplified Bible

The Jezebel-Ahab principality enters the
rooms of unforgiveness
and turns them into a fortress-of-wrong-thinking,
that raises an arrogant fist against knowing
the Real God, LOVE.
(2 Cor. 10:4)

THE FRUIT
of bitterness is pain twisted into malice,
injustice turned to religous legalism,
sin changed into explanations for evil.

Bitterness is literal poison
that thrusts a root into your heart from which
corruption of integrity grows until
it bears the fruit of outright evil.

one more satisfactory, more indulgent.
"greed which is idolatry."
Col.3:5

Greed summons the Jezebel-spirit which fans
the flame of greed into burning **jealousy**
of all the blessings of others.
Remember Naboth and his vineyard?
For his prosperity and the blessing of God, he lost his life.
Jealousy *is* murder.

Wherever the pride-of-greed lives, jealousy moves in.
And **jealousy** is sure evidence of Jezebel-in-residence.

Jealousy is the madness of Satan whose
envy of God cost him his position *with* God.
To harbor **jealousy** is to live dangerously
close to the enemy's corruption
and therefore... in God's displeasure.

Jesus was murdered by bitter jealousy.
His spiritual power, His popularity, His stunning wisdom;
these, His spiritual blessings, the religious
could not tolerate.
So out of envy, they instigated His murder.
*"For he (Pilate) knew it was out of envy that they had
handed Jesus over to him."*
Matt. 27:18

Of all forms of envy, spiritual envy is the most vicious.
To walk in the favor of God and wear His mark of blessing
is to evoke the most terrible and murderous rage of hell.

Jezebel is the messenger Hate sends to deliver his fury...
his own continuing jealousy of God.

James, brother of Jesus, must have fully understood
the evil of jealousy. He wrote the great expose' of it,
naming selfish ambition as the root of murder.
"But if you harbor bitter envy and selfish ambition in your
hearts, do not boast about it or deny the truth.
Such 'wisdom' does not come down from heaven
but is earthly, unspiritual, of the devil.
For where you have envy and selfish ambition,
there you find disorder and every evil practice."
James 3:14-16

TAKE DOWN THE TREE:
The only solution for Jezebel/Ahab evil.
But the tree cannot be trimmed or bent,
nor can it be *cut* down.
The tree of jezebel-evil must be savagely uprooted,
and the root of *hatred for God,*
utterly thrust into the Light.

When describing the coming "work" of the Spirit,
John the Baptist spoke of the axe.
"The axe is already laid at the root of the trees;
therefore every tree that does not bear good fruit
is cut down and thrown into the fire."
Matt. 3:10

The "axe to the root" is a violent act, the nature of
it is upheaval and destruction, dirt and wreckage.

Savage blows often come to the slaves of Jezebel-Ahab
    in the form of a prophet with an axe of blank truth,
        plunged straight into your heart.

The hardness of a Jezebeled-heart is settled cement. Only a
great blow can open a chink for God's mercy to enter and solve.

The Holy Spirit can go to that malignant root.
        He can search your heart and find the poison
           you have hidden from yourself.

Prayer invites Him – this precious All-Knowing Spirit –
    into the chambers of your alienated soul.
        Desperate prayer brings intervention of the Spirit,
    and that is precisely what it takes to escape
        Satan's captivity in Jezebel-hate.

James, by the Spirit, gave us the solution to jealousy:
  "Submit yourselves, then, to God. Resist the devil, and he will
  flee from you. Come near to God and he will come near to
  you. Wash your hands, you sinners, and purify your hearts,
    you double-minded. Grieve, mourn and wail.
  Change your laughter to mourning and your joy to gloom.
  Humble yourselves before the Lord, and He will lift you up."
                James 4:7-10

The evil-fruited tree will one day be "cut down and thrown
    into the fire" of God's inescapable judgment.
May we welcome the deep blows of His mercy now
    so the tree of Hate's planting will come out of our hearts!
      "Before that Great and Terrible Day of the Lord."

The Mind of Evil

Jezebel/Ahab live in *the mind,* not the human spirit;
 in a thought life that broods only on SELF.
By obsession with your own wants,
 by excessive love and pity for yourself,
 you call for that demonic presence and power
to get for you what your greed demands.

The dangerous delusion is the arrogance of believing
 that **anything you think is the truth and
 anything you want is God's will.**

You make yourself center of the universe
around which all must revolve and to which all matters relate.
 By such coddled selfishness, you are "god" on the tower.
 And by that presumption Satan takes you over
  because your self-worship is really of... him.
Self-defending thoughts
  are the constant voice from hell
  that excuses, exalts and exonerates... YOU.

First, you must know that you have USED that spirit
 for this purpose: to get your way,
deliberately, by a long series of unethical choices.

Here are some of the delusions – flattering but heinous lies –
 that nestle in the mind, made sick by selfishness:

What you want is automatically God's will and
   your "sacred right."
Your thoughts are consumed with what-you-want and
   anything you want is what-you-deserve
      either because you have **given** and purchased it
      or because you have **suffered** so much
   that God *and* people owe you a rich compensation.

You don't have to abide by any standard of integrity or holiness,
   but others do! And the standard to which they must
      adhere is determined by... *you.*
   You make the laws for your world and all who live in it.
   But you yourself are exempt from adherence to them.

You live with continuous inner rage over which
   you have no remorse because it is justified
   by the failure and misdirection of
those in your world who should meet your needs.

You do not feel you are wrong, *they* are.
But at the same time, you live with an inward and private
torment of screaming voices and the rehearsal of violent
arguments that never happened – invented
conflicts and fantasies
   of personal affronts
      that leave you divided from, and bitter with,
         your world...

You are driven by a busy imagination,
   full of private lusts and indulgences,
      all of which are kept as secret as you can make them.

You spiritualize your desires and lusts and motives into
　　valid issues that come from God,
　and you create a justified purpose for those sins and
　assign them to God's will others are to perform... for you.

This is your belief: others should not only DO what you say
　　because you "know," but as well should "be" what you say.
And your endless frustration and dissatisfaction is because
　　they never live up to your idea.

You know what's best and how it should all be done.
　　Just do it your way. There is no other.

Underlying all this twisted thinking are serious flaws
of character by the ***complete absence of fear of God,***
　　or the knowledge of His Holy Government.

By the fear of the Lord we are kept from evil.
Jezebel dwells with those who fear Satan and
　　have no fear of God.

But the presence of evil spirits is not the real problem nor
　　is deliverance the first solution to Jezebel.
For the problem was, in the beginning, one of the will,
　　of choice... of **sin**... of personal and deliberate rebellion.

You chose to give up integrity for self-serving ends,
　　and the recovery of integrity is the wrenching work
　　　　you must do.

You invited Jezebel-domain over your soul and
welcomed the evil spirits to serve **your** purpose.

Problem: they turned on you, Satan and his black angels
    tricked you by the slithering promise to help you
    get your way, but they secured THEIR way over your life.

*"For though we walk (live) in the flesh, we are not
carrying on our warfare according to the flesh and using
mere human weapons.*
*For the weapons of our warfare are not physical [weapons
of flesh and blood], but they are mighty before God for the
overthrow and destruction of strongholds,*
*[Inasmuch as we] refute arguments and theories and
reasonings and every proud and lofty thing that sets itself
up against the [true] knowledge of God; and we lead every
thought and purpose away captive into the obedience of
Christ (the Messiah, the Anointed One), being in readiness
to punish every [insubordinate for his] disobedience, when
your own submission and obedience [as a church] are fully
secured and complete."*
2 Cor. 10:4 Amplified Bible

The fight is one of surrendering the mind to God,
    allowing Him to take over by the Holy Spirit,
coming to focus with the mind on God's voice and not
    on the lusts of self.

"For those who are according to the flesh and are controlled by its unholy desires set their minds on and pursue those things which gratify the flesh, but those who are according to the Spirit and are controlled by the desires of the Spirit set their minds on and seek those things which gratify the [Holy] Spirit."
Romans 8:5 Amplified Bible

The weapons of our warfare are mighty to the pulling down of strongholds. Praise God!

You can bring your mind under the Light of God's Truth by claiming the cleansing blood of Christ and declaring the defeat of Jezebel-lies.

Chariot of Fire

A future chariot of fire
will catch up the Elijahs of tomorrow
for the same spectacular ride to glory.

Training Elisha

An essential part of defeating Jezebel and Ahab
    is to equip your successors for a
        victory greater than your own.

The person who cares for God
    passes the baton to the next runner,
    giving away all the hard won secrets to
        the next generation.

And that fresh courier steps on the stage of
    the drama ready to go
        quite beyond the teacher.

What Elijah fought with agony,
    Elisha soared through with triumph.

Elijah cleared the rugged path for Elisha
    in bleak labor but also grand adventure
        to learn who God is… and isn't,
    by suffering and by triumph.

Elijah spent his last moments, opened his own journey,
        nurturing Elisha in the lessons – not of principles –
        but in the power of the God
          they shared and served together.

"Thus the saying 'One sows and another reaps' is true.
I sent you to reap what you have not worked for.
Others have done the hard work and you have
reaped the benefits of their work."

John 4:37

Elisha was twice as grand for God,
    having double the power,
    and greater the scope.

But it is Elijah who will return to usher in the
    Son, to tear down mountains and
    make His way clear.

It was Elijah on the mount with Jesus.

    The courage of the pioneers is noted by God.
    Their toil to break open ground-never-plowed
        so that others may sow and reap
            is a priceless first fruit,
                enjoyed by God.

Elijah Raptured

*"… [s]uddenly a chariot of fire appeared with
horses of fire which separated the two of them;
and Elijah went up by a whirlwind into heaven."*
2 Kings 2:11 NKJ

Elijah was no longer bound to the earth of Jezebel's despotism.
Though her reign was intact,
   the kingdom of his recognition
      was not threatened by it, nor involved in it…

Elijah had moved to the timeless future and
   all of its unimagined glory
      within the Father's Unshakable Command.

He became a soaring prophet
   propelled into another age,
   no longer living by his own era.

He had been a prophet of the natural earth:
   of predicting drought and rain.
He had served as prophet of heaven's idea:
   calling down the fire of judgment.

Now he saw not just the future, but God's
   eternal salvation in its far distance.
   And he hurled it by that vision
      down to the earthly Now.

Ultimate victory over Jezebel was centuries away.
    But in calling Jehu forth,
      Elijah brought that future event
        backward into Israel's day.

The Lamb was slain *before* the foundations of the earth.
Those in the Old Testament who saw Him,
    lived in the timeless victory of it.

Elijah had defeated the Ahab/Jezebel conspiracy –
    not by sword but by **vision**.

The vision of God: Eternal and Unchanging.
When his eye left the focus on evil and tyranny
and was fixed on the Father in His Ultimate Rest,
then… then! Elijah soared to the heavens.

He had lived in awareness of
    heaven's timeless dominion and
    the throne's splendor
  long before the chariot of fire
  carried him to the familiar home of his spirit.

He had transcended the violent conflict over earth's throne
    and dwelled in the sweep of God's Eternal Triumph,
    where there is no disturbance and no disorder.
      And… no rebellion that can last.

The Rapture of a fiery chariot was natural to Elijah.
    No surprise.

He knew heaven's plans because he knew heaven,
   by abiding in its Throne Room.

2 Kings 2

Elijah was not in a nervous state waiting for his rapture.
When he was taken up, he was gently moving,
   walking the path of God's assignment,
   quietly nurturing his disciple,
but more aware of heaven than earth.

More on the Other Side than in this murky one.

Knowing full well his glorious departure,
   (unique in the annals of God),
      he didn't stop living his duty nor
      did he sit down in some
      self-conscious state of religious superiority.

Ever the friend of God's Lofty Purpose,
   in the humility of a servant,
   he was preparing his successor... not to succeed him,
      but to **exceed** him!

*"Then it happened as they [Elijah and Elisha]
continued on and talked, that
suddenly a chariot of fire appeared
with horses of fire and separated the two of them,
and Elijah went up in a whirlwind into heaven."*

2 Kings 2:11 NKJ

Now the secret...

Jesus was pictured in Jehu, the hint of
   His Kingly zeal and triumph.
But Jesus also is seen in Elijah.
   Jesus Christ, the One True Prophet,
   who would perform only "what He sees the Father do."
                  John 5:19

The Character of the Son rested on Elijah.
And only by that Pure and Faithful Character
– dwelling in the depths of *your spirit* –
   will you transcend the prince of this world,
   call forth the defeat of Jezebel-lawlessness
      by a vision of the Glorious Cross,
   and soar to the heavens by the chariot
     of your own Rapture.

The Future Rapture.

Mount of Transfiguration

"As [Jesus] prayed, the appearance of His face was altered,
and His robe became white and glistening.
And behold, two men talked with Him,
who were __Moses__ __and__ __Elijah__, who appeared in glory
and spoke of His decease
which He was about to accomplish at Jerusalem."
Luke 9:29-31 (Emphasis Mine)

Such was the importance of Elijah's mantle that
he was an ongoing presence in the New Testament of
Jesus' walk on earth.

Moses and Elijah shared a common human experience.
Neither were able to finish their tough assignment from God,
and both had to pass the baton of the race to a successor
whose easy achievement overshadowed
even their unusual splendor.

Moses, minister of the Law, died in mountain terrain with
a never-found grave. He could see the Promised Land of his
tedious striving, but he had to die and get out of the way of
Joshua, who – in the silence of faith –
simply walked in.

Elijah, prophet of God's will, soared by chariot straight to
heaven while Jezebel bullied from her corrupt throne.
He heard about, but didn't participate in, the anointing of
Jehu, who toppled with a word, the queen Elijah
couldn't dethrone.

Moses had no part in the conquering of the Promised land.
　　Joshua had the faith Moses did not possess.

Elijah didn't anoint Jehu, nor ever met him.
　　　Another prophet did that.
　　Jehu had the authority Elijah never had.

Two men (Moses and Elijah) humanity would rate as failures,
given a place of honor witnessing and even sharing in the glory
of Jesus' coming victory over death and human sin. Why them?

The Old Testament is full of living pictures drawn by vivid
stories that speak of eternal truths. Moses and Elijah, the best
of humanity, faithful in God's service. Theirs was a colossal
effort, valiant and steady, but they were just human,
　　and by that limitation, unable to finish their task for God.

They stand as willing servants, but they represent principles:
　　anointing, empowerment and relationship with God.
　　Those would seem to be enough… but it isn't.
　　Humanity at its best. Fatally short of the Mark.

The Law and its glory: Moses
The Prophetic and its authority: Elijah.
　　The best but… not enough.

Joshua and Jehu, conquerors with ease.
　　They were merely a shadow pointing to
　　　the Reality, Jesus Christ.

Jesus, the only Finisher of God's Dream called man.
Jesus, the only completion of God's ideas,
    the sole victor over God's enemy.

No person, however empowered could conquer, finish... obey!
        But Jesus! Jesus finished all.
        And He completed all for them – for us.
        And all is finished now because He performed it.
        It is finished.

Moses saw in the distance the Promise of Prosperity.
    "Moses... wrote of me." John 5:46
Elijah saw in the future the Defeat of Evil.
    "Jehu will kill... "   1 Kings 19:17

What they glimpsed far away and above them,
    was the Son of God,
        Only True Conqueror of realms and kings.

Though killed by Jehu, Jezebel really remained undefeated.
    She appears wherever God appears.
Down through the ages, right into the scene of Jesus' world,
    Jezebel never was completely conquered.

Though Joshua conquered and lived in The Land of Plenty,
        his descendants lost it entirely.
The "types and shadows" failed in the end.

Our Father Which Art in Heaven sent His Son, His ONLY Son,
  to possess with unshakable permanence
    the Home of Our Inheritance.
And Jesus Christ destroyed Jezebel so she can never rise
    again against His Holy Blood.
  She only lives if we swallow the lie of her power.

Moses and Elijah came to see their personal victory,
  their individual calling, their successful completion –
    all, all rested on this Dazzling Son,
    transfigured before them into
    not just His Original Splendor, but that
    Exceeding never-before-seen Glory yet to come!
      What joy!
    What personal vindication secured by
      Another!

And what they saw on that Mount was the Cross!
What the disciples saw in Jesus – Son of God, yes –
    was only earthly thrones, amazing power.

These Old Testament servants shared in the mesmerizing glory
  of His Coming Triumph and spoke together of what
    that Phenomenal Completion would cost!

      His imminent death!

The Law of God's Holiness satisfied and
      the Prophecy of Christ's Victory fulfilled,

Moses and Elijah, who had before yielded to a superior man,
now yielded their offices – Law and Prophet –

to this Supreme One

over all, before all, and forever... *All*.

"This is My Beloved Son. Hear Him!"
Luke 9:35

Chariot of Fire

The New Testament in its abbreviated form
    is explained in picture-detail by
      events of the past,
    by stories of the Old Testament.

The "Old" explaining the "New"
      before ever it was.
    Amazing Author! telling the end
     before the beginning.
    Giving the Answer before the Question.

*   *   *   *

Every enlightened believer of every age
    has lived under the shadow of
    the soon return of Jesus.

Paul believed it was imminent.
He had to believe that
    because FOR HIM
      it was!

And so today, the Watchful live in
     "perhaps-it-will-be-soon."
      As they should!

They are wise, who live under the
    awesome specter of Jesus' Return.

Only one life-span, one flicker of breath –
    to cultivate eternity!

We are preparing every moment for an
    infinite destiny, sowing our immortal seeds
      in a permanent furrow for a
      harvest of Forever.

Jesus is coming for His Bride in a Sure Event of the future.
    Those of the Church Past
    who adored His Appearing and
    prepared to meet Him
    will rise first from their grave of sleep.

> *"[t]he dead in Christ shall rise first."*
> 1 Thess. 4:16

And those alive who love Him with Undying Love
    will suddenly rise like a magnet – drawn by longing –
    to meet HIM in the clouds.

> *"One will be taken and one left."*
> Matt. 24:40

It is called the *Rapture* and Elijah is an
    explanation of it.

Enoch and Elijah, raptured first;
    their lives are answers to the question,
      "What does it take to be included in the Rapture?"

"Enoch walked with God and was not for God took him."
Gen. 5:24

Amos asked the question:
"How can two walk together except they be agreed"
Amos 3:3 KJV

You can only walk with God by complete agreement with Him.
By the waiver of all your disagreements.

God is ever in His Creative Move.
He has His Rhythmic Sway
and you may join Him but only by the abandon
of your favorite path…

To walk with Him, you must move as He moves.
The Wind of His Course blows north and
it blows south;
a breath of warmth and a gale of cold.

Walk is movement… thrust and courage.

Jesus *walked* with God and could spend long days
just waiting for that "Hallowed Move."
John 11:6

Or He could flow with the Winds of Heaven
and change His entire course
in a second of new understanding.

One minute He refused to attend the Feast,
the next, He was there... teaching.
(John 7:1-14)

To *walk with Go*d is a phenomenal thing.
It is surrender of the deepest kind...
and the most rare.

Then... to walk *with* God. With Him – is intimacy.
With Him, sweet word of oneness.

So Enoch-of-the-First-Rapture answers us this:
rapture is about intimate surrender,
union and movement.

Enoch simply... disappeared. Quietly lost into God.

But Elijah,
carried off by a public chariot of fire
and horses ablaze –
he speaks a different answer to
the question, Rapture.

Fraught with blood and war,
Elijah walked in many Fires.
His words were fire,
his ministry, flame.
He declared the Blazing Judgment.

The God of Elijah was lightning, fire, and smoke.
And Elijah was His minister of burning zeal.

Defeating Jezebel was Elijah's task and
   when it was completed by God's pleasure,
      the chariot came.

Because he brought the Fire of Heaven
     down on earthly evil,
   that same Fire of Heaven carried him to the Throne:
      origin of All Fire.

Enoch was REST.
Elijah was WAR.
     Two elements, two conditions of Rapture.

There are seven churches of Revelation. (Rev. 2-3)
   They tell us of:
   seven issues of life,
   seven weaknesses of man,
     seven tests from God and
       fourteen golden rewards.
   God gives double for our trials.

The rewards are conditional.
   They must be earned by obedient following.
   They must be gained by the strain of a warrior
     engaging the enemy – within; without.

The most fiery test, with the severest judgments,
is the crucible of Jezebel. (Rev. 2:18-29)

Every believer will face the test of Jezebel
and upon its agony rests your eternal position.

The Bride is nurtured in a secret glade of those
Overriding Wings.
But she is charged with a mission of
war against evil and for that,
the courage of a zealot is required.

To reign with Christ through Eternity,
the Bride must conquer Jezebel-Satan.
This is her training for ruling.

The reward of this conquest is to govern nations,
to be counted fit to bear the authority of God
by the proven willingness to stand unwavering
against evil, against God's mortal enemy.

In the end, it is simply... the conquest of your own fear
by letting God swallow it for you.

Jezebel can rule only over subjects-in-fear.
Those she cannot intimidate have beaten her
and have overcome that vapid evil
by the fierceness of a God-imparted courage
in uncompromising loyalty.
Like Elijah.

And these are willing flames of God's holiness,
walking torches of His Love and Jealousy,
sent to blaze a path of purity for
His Son's Triumphant Return.

Vessels of flame, set afire *By* God, *For* God.

Blazing as stars forever.

The Mantle

"And it came about when the Lord was about to take up
Elijah by a whirlwind to heaven,
that Elijah went with Elisha from Gilgal.
Elijah said to Elisha, 'Stay here please… '
But Elisha said, 'As the Lord lives and
as you yourself live, I will not leave you.'"
2 Kings 2:1,2

At Gilgal… at Bethel… at Jericho,
Elijah bid his servant stay.
Three times he gave the command, but
Elisha would not be dismissed.
He refused to miss this final splendor.
The passion of his heart for Elijah's
spiritual genius made him
determined…
fiercely tenacious.
Unmovable.

The Father watched the obsession for the divine
that drove Elisha and it pleased Him.

"Elijah took his mantle and folded it together and
struck the waters, and they were divided here and there,
so that the two of them crossed over on dry ground."

Going from Israel into Ammon,
    crossing from the
comfort of earth's home into the wilderness of solitude,
    Elijah was fully leaving all his world
      and its attaching cords.

Elisha – willing to go even there.

"Now it came about when they had crossed over,
that Elijah said to Elisha,
'Ask what I shall do for you before I am taken from you.'"
2 Kings 2:8,9

Elisha had followed and watched the great man,
    knew his magnificence came from deep within
    the depths of his spirit, a spirit that
      transcended all things human… and
      even… all things Elijah.

Simply put, he had to have it, whatever it was.
    He had seen something so vital,
    so necessary that he pressed and pushed to have it.
    Shamelessly and precisely he wanted a

"double portion of his spirit."

Elisha asked for the intangible…
    double portion of the man's *spirit*!
    Not his power, not his knowledge.

A person's spirit is the hidden essence of his very being.
The place where his secret lives.
Elisha yearned for that secret,
    that treasured mystery of Elijah!

He [Elijah] said, "you have asked a hard thing.
Nevertheless, if you see me when I am taken from you,
it shall be so for you, but if not, it shall not be so."
                verse 10

Elijah, possessed by God to the
    absolute end of himself,
        could promise or give nothing,
            as nothing was his.
Not even his spiritual wealth.

And Elisha, challenged to push forward
    yet another mile of following... of pursuing.
Joined Elijah in the wilderness of nothing-but-God.
    All in preparation for the "secret."

"Then it came about as they were going along and talking,
    that behold, there appeared a chariot of fire
and horses of fire which separated the two of them,
    and Elijah went up by a whirlwind to heaven."

"Elisha saw it and cried out, 'My father, my father,
    the chariots of Israel and its horsemen!'"

*"Then he took hold of his own clothes and tore them in
two pieces. He also took up the mantle
of Elijah… "*

Taking the garments of his individuality,
    tearing apart his very identity
        by a self imposed violence,
dividing in two his soul's pride from his spirit's hunger,
he wrung out the grief of humility so he could receive this
    descending garment… another man's victory.

    Perhaps what floated down from the
        blaze of Elijah's whirlwind,
            from sky to earth,
    was the **prayer shawl of Elijah.**

    The Elijah mantle was the garment of prayer,
        his intimacy with the Father.
    And from within that private union came
        his awesome authority.

    ***The secret of Elijah*,**
the Jewish prayer shawl under which the man
covered himself for communion.

Through prayer, Elijah had gained all.
    By prayer he literally lived
        and also found *himself*.
Prayer was his focus, his strength.

The double portion of the Elijah-spirit was
that prayer life.
He hid himself inside the shawl,
tasseled with authority
and embroidered with scripture.

The power of God was there
infused *into* him by secret oneness…
by the unseen harmony
of a symphony with the Father,
a concert that made Elijah an
instrument of that Father's Extravagant Passion
for His poor children.

The New Testament memorial of Elijah, the
secret clearly given to Jesus' brother, James…

*"the fervent, effectual prayer of
a righteous man."*
James 5:16 KJV

*"He [Elisha] took the mantle of Elijah that fell from
him and struck the waters and said,
'Where is the Lord, the God of Elijah?'"*

A great cry, a wail of agonized desire to know
the Magnificent God of Elijah.
Elisha would live without Elijah, but he
could no longer survive without
the same Lord GOD.

"And when he also had struck the waters, they were divided here and there; and Elisha crossed over."

Exactly as Elijah's prayers had opened his own way
by the miracle of heaven's dominion,
Elisha stepped back across into Israel to face
the anguished world for God.

He crossed the Jordan River that lay between the
wilderness and the kingdom.
He had picked up the heaven-touched mantle that
floated down and took up the same
intimate life of prayer.

He used that mantle-power of the secret:
absolute dependence on prayer
to walk through the river of death-to-self,
and heal lepers, conquer poison,
raise dead children,

with exactly *double* the number of miracles
as his Prophet Elijah.

Epilogue

Elijah, being the shadow of Christ
means **yo**u, His Elisha-Church,
are meant for the "double portion"
of His Spirit…

Vessels Only

We are clay pots, earthen vessels[1] only,
   bearing the spirit of another entity.
   The question is WHO has you?
      WHO speaks to and through you?
         WHO?

There are only two answers…
   two Spirit Beings in the universe.
   God the True and Satan the Lie.

"Now in a large house there are not only
gold and silver vessels,
*but also **vessels of wood and of earthenware**,*
and some to honor and some to dishonor.
Therefore, if anyone cleanses himself from these things,
*he will be **a vessel for honor**, sanctified, useful to the*
Master, prepared for every good work."
2 Timothy 2:20,21   NASB

Peter spoke directly out from the Father in heaven
   one minute, but the next
   he was Satan's literal mouthpiece.
   He heard, agreed and therefore carried
     the whisper of
   self-saving-avoidance-of-the-cross:
     the Religion of Hell.

[1] 2 Cor. 4:7

Jesus knew exactly on both occasions
    the identity behind the words.
    The first, from the Father in Heaven. 1
    And the next, from Satan himself 2

We are capable of going from one master
    to Another the false to the Real.

Anyone at any time can speak out from Jezebel-influence.
    It is a matter of values.
    Control calls "Jezebel" to your side.
    Relinquishment sends her running.

    Resentment of God beckons Jezebel to
        fan the flames of your private bitterness.
    Surrender to God by faith in His goodness,
        repels that satanic being.
    Pride and religion are her forte and she
    moves in wherever these are indulged.
    Humility and the genuine are unbearable
        to Satan's Jezebel-guise.

To constantly drink with "Jezebel" thinking is to
    become drunk with her illegitimate power
        and wield it as a force of witchcraft
        against those you toast with her ideas.

[1] Matt. 16:17
[2] Matt. 16:23, Mark 8:33

Vessel of Jezebel. Never owned by her.
A voluntary slave you are.
However unwitting, no matter how blind,
    "Jezebel" requires consent and agreement.
    She will take up residence only by
        sinful invitation.

The one who survives the inevitable fire of
        Jezebel-presence
            will emerge
        a vessel of golden honor,
        fit to embody *and* radiate the
        Very Master of Glory.

Out of the Web

Jezebel will tempt you into a wrestling entanglement,
    a futile struggle to "change" the person in evil.
A web of lies will spin its circles and catch you in
    its complex confusion.
This maze of strange ideas you are tempted to solve,
    and so you are caught in the web.

You will grapple in the ring with humanity, only to
    be pinned to the mat by humiliating defeat.

    "But we do not wrestle against flesh and blood... "
                       Ephesians 6:12

    It's not a person you meet. It is either God or Satan.
    Part of the Evil Plan is to get you
    enmeshed in a human war.

You cannot reason with a demon,
    nor engage in debates of truth with a Liar.

If you will follow God
there can be no relationship with a person
who consistently gives in to the Jezebel-sins.

Leave any fight. Get out of any relationship
    with such a one... till they are free.

If flight is impossible, then become non-involved.

Have no more involvement than you would
    with a store clerk.
To the store clerk you pay what you owe, no more.
    To the store clerk you exchange pleasantries,
        but not philosophy.
    You give courtesy and respect,
    but not your "unlisted" phone number.

Blood and Victory

Many call on the Blood of Jesus who do not
acknowledge the sins for which the Blood was spilled.

Repentance is the key to get out of "Jezebel."
And repentance is total responsibility for your
"thoughts, words, and deeds done in the body."

Human nature slides toward blame instead of
naked accountability.

But remember Ahab was held accountable for
all he allowed Jezebel to perform.

God's standard is inescapable and that His
wrath rests on the disobedient   (Col. 3:6)
is absolute. Believer as well as nonbeliever.

It is the Blood of the Lamb alone that assuages His
abhorrence of sin. And that Blood, that precious Blood,
is absolutely satisfying to His Holy Eye.

The Blood of the Lamb is available only to the admitted sinner
and it is the dread and nightmare of "Jezebel."
The blood of Jesus Christ is your covering
protection, your sanctity and safety.

The Blood must cover your sins of Jezebel and Ahab.
And God – your Abba – will reveal them to
the willing listener.

Praying for Rain

When our life is noted and recorded in
    Time's Memory,
  will it be remembered as a Life of secret Prayer?
  Prayer that squeezes rain out of a dry heaven
    and waters a land scorched by sin?

For all you could say about Elijah –
    his faith, his anointing, his fire –
  what is Written and Preserved is the
    bald essence of his life,
  the meaning of the story and the way it all happened:
    fervent, ***effectual prayer.***

The tests of walking with God are all designed for
  one end, really… to press you into Him.

    How He desires communion!
  How He longs to sit in the Big Chair as Father
    and hear our infant-cry…
  to whisper eternal secrets in our ear and
    solve unsolvable quandaries.

Prayer is how Heaven remembers Elijah's life. [1]
    "he prayed earnestly"
  Prayer of such intimacy and rapport with God
    as to touch His strange ideas
  and then to be the open conduit through which
    they flowed to earth.

[1] James 5:17

It takes a miracle to liberate a single person, or
   an entire land of the scourge of Jezebel.
   A miracle is something only God can do.

In the final education of overcoming,
    prayer is the total answer for
      helpless humanity...
Only prayer, *only* prayer brings in the miracle.

Prayer discovers the problem and the plan.
And prayer brings it into visibility.

What is prayer? Prayer is asking questions more than
     making requests,
     silence more than speaking...
     Prayer is relationship with the Divine.
     Relationship!
Prayer is profound listening to Another by
    the sacrifice of time lavished on seeking.

To give no time is to hear no secrets.

And to give up in the face of tyranny is to
    miss your appointment with
    the Author of your Destiny.

You Will Know Them

Jezebel will invade the Church wherever Christ is rising,
and contend to replace His Voice and Throne,
motivated by the raging jealousy
of ambition.

Jesus soberly warned us of the need to be
wise as serpents, innocent as doves.

*"Behold, I am sending you out like
sheep in the midst of wolves:
be wary and wise as serpents,
and be innocent (harmless, guileless,
and without falsity) as doves."*
Matt. 10:16 Amplified Bible

But the Jezebel-spirit is brilliantly religious,
clever to hide in a mask of the admirable.
Appearing in the mild goodness of a sheep.
So how can you know if you are dealing with
the evil of Satan by the name of Jezebel?

*"Beware of the false prophets, who come to you in
sheep's clothing, but
inwardly are ravenous wolves.
You will know them by their fruits."*
Matt. 7:15,16a NAS

Sometimes you don't know.
In due time the fruit appears.
Your spirit is troubled without an answer as to why
the words and actions don't match.

The test of a person's authenticity, the measure
of their true spirituality,
is not miracles, not power.
Not brilliance, nor knowledge.

The litmus test is **character**. Not human goodness,
but the unhuman **attributes of Christ**.
Fruit, not religious blab. Fruit, not phenomenon.

Fruit is of the Spirit... only.

"The fruit of the (Holy) Spirit
(the work which His presence within accomplishes)
is love, joy (gladness), peace, patience
(an even temper, forbearance), kindness,
goodness (benevolence) faithfulness."
Gal. 5:22 Amplified Bible (Emphasis Mine)

This is the character of Jesus Christ infused into
a believer by
deep humility and surrender.

Jezebel fruit?

*"Now the deeds of the flesh are evident, which are
immorality, impurity, sensuality, idolatry, sorcery, enmities,
strife, jealousy, outbursts of anger,
disputes, dissensions, factions, envying, drunkenness,
carousing and things like these
of which I forewarn you just as I have forewarned you
that those who practice such things
shall not inherit the kingdom of God."*
Gal. 5:19-21 NAS

The one-in-Jezebel bears the evil fruit
a heavy burden strapping your soul,
an unbearable weight of
"religious law."

This will always
lower you under inferiority and
breed in you suspicion of God.
Jezebel severs your connection with His love
and by unshakable mastery,
takes His place to define you,
to control you.
And above all, frighten you.

Demonic assault is released to beat and bombard,
your soul with vicious
blows that can neither be explained nor proven...
because of and coming through
one who operates in the brutality of Satan's Jezebel.

The words may be flawless in doctrine,
religiously right.
But what comes from it?
Confusion or truth?
Division or unity?
Blessing or cursing?
Faith or fear?

The fruit Jezebel spews on your soul is
despair, hopelessness, and rejection,
all of which are the fruits of terror.

If these poisons come from a relationship in
your life, begin to seek God to
name Jezebel Himself.
Be not quick to name it; let Him.
He will!

*"A good tree cannot bear bad fruit,
and a bad tree cannot bear good fruit.
Every tree that does not bear good fruit is
cut down and thrown into the fire.
So then, you will know them by their fruits."*
Matt. 7:15-20 NAS (Emphasis mine)

Queen of Heaven

For all her destruction, for all her undermining
    of holiness and integrity,
Jezebel is merely a forerunner of that which
    is even more heinous to God...
A principality called the "queen of heaven."

Israel struggled for centuries with Baal worship.
Eventually, their spiritual weakness was such
    that they began to worship
    what their forefathers never worshiped.

> *"... they have forsaken Me and have
> made this an alien place and have
> burned sacrifices in it to other gods
> that neither they nor their forefathers
> nor the kings of Judah had ever known..."*
> Jer. 19:4

This "queen of heaven" was the
    Assyro-Babylonian goddess, Ishtar.

By the time of Jeremiah,
    this demonic ruler was
    worshiped by entire families.
        Even children were serving it.

"The children gather wood,
and the fathers kindle the fire, and
the women knead dough to make cakes
for the queen of heaven; and they pour
out libations to other gods in order to spite Me."
Jer. 7:18 NAS

Jezebel says, "worship MY god."
But the queen of heaven says, "I am god."
Jezebel leads astray from God, but
the queen of heaven takes God's place.

The nation had fallen to a state of ruin
that Jehovah would no longer endure.

Jeremiah, told to pray for them no more,
warned of God's sure judgment:

"So I will hurl you out of this land
into the land which you have not known,
neither you nor your fathers;
and there you will serve other gods
day and night, for I shall grant you no favor."
Jer. 16:13

Prophets warned the nation about Baal
worship, but when the
queen of heaven
became the idol of the whole family
and all believed in her,
it was finished for Judah and
terrible judgment fell.

God will tolerate and strive with us when
we wander away from Him, but
He rises in holy indignation when
someone with the evil spirit
"queen of heaven" takes His place
in our lives...
and we allow it.

The nation was not merely punished with
catastrophe... it fell to the hands of
Nebuchadnezzar of Babylon.

It was destroyed and the people were
given over to Babylonian
captivity under this cruel, heathen king.

King Zedekiah, who tried to escape, was
captured – as Jeremiah had said – and
blinded after watching his sons murdered.
Then he was chained and taken to Babylon.

The palaces were burned,
    the walls of Jerusalem destroyed,
    the nobles slain.

And most of the people were taken away
    to be slaves.

When a church, a family, or a nation capitulates to the
    "queen of heaven"
    it is inevitable – unavoidable –
    that the judgment of a Jealous God
        will sent a terrible punishment.
        And prayer cannot turn it around.

And that is so *today*, not only *then*.

Resist Not

Jezebel requires a vessel to ride into this world.
She must have a human means willing to give her free rein.

Under New Testament grace, we must clearly separate
the evil power of the air from its human vessel.

To the Master of Evil, we are told to resist
and to do so with vigor.
But to the human who bears this evil,
we have a mandate to resist… NOT.

*"Do not resist the evil man [who injures you]
but if anyone strikes you on the right jaw or cheek,
turn to him the other too…
But I tell you, Love your enemies and
pray for those who persecute you…
To show that you are children of your
Father Who is in heaven.
For He makes His sun rise on
the wicked and on the good, and makes the rain
fall upon the upright and the wrongdoers [alike]."*
Matt. 5:39,44,45 Amplified Bible

"Resist not" is the command of Wisdom:
let the person have their choice of evil, and its
inevitable consequences.
Do not pick up a futile struggle with a will that is
firmly set on iniquity and prefers delusion to reality.

The use of Jezebel power, a power that is satanic, is a decision.
The one in Jezebel did not stumble into demonic evil.
It is evil by deliberate preference,
not an accident of ignorance.

Those in Jezebel-evil have foolishly *chosen evil*.
They are not captured prisoners nor innocent victims.
Evil is a step-by-step decision of irresponsibility,
the suicide of integrity.

You cannot fight a person's choice.
It is a sacred gift from God,
one He will not violate nor withdraw.
We choose. We always choose.
Who you are is what you have decided to be.
Where you end is where you chose to arrive,
deliberately, consciously.

The Love of God is absolute freedom,
a freedom so total that we cannot
take it in nor copy it.
The gift of following or rejecting Him
is unequivacal freedom.

God even gives us the liberty to abuse Him,
misrepresent Him; reject Him.
Not only does God give the choice,
He supports it when it is chosen.
This life is simply about choices.
All can choose. All *do* choose.

Jezebel-wickedness wants you to tussle with
the person's will, to exert precious energy
    figuring out their schemes.
    Striving to change their thinking and their choice.

Choice was the *path* *i*n to Jezebel and
    choice is the *way out*.

Choice is an entirely solitary work.
Every person does it alone, in secret.
And God alone knows if the choice
    toward His Lordship is genuine.

Christ Himself did not fight the evil of Rome,
    nor strive to make the religious leaders see.
He hid His truths from them in the parables.
His escape from evil was that He was simply uninvolved.
    Mentally, emotionally, He was God's.

Jesus left strife, walked away from arguments.
Those endless demands of the religious that
Jesus explain His actions and justify His words
    were merely a smokescreen of confusion,
        meant to blame *Hi*m
    for their own failure to acknowledge that
        He was indeed… God.
    "He did not convince *me!*"

Jezebel is after converts.
She is a contagious disease and when you struggle to change
a Jezebel-person, you are tempted to use the tactics of Jezebel:
 rage, hatred, tyranny, rejection, obsession.
To strive to change an evil person is to become evil
 because it is a violation of their sacred choice.

One who wants God *will* choose God.
One who wants self *will* choose self
 and it consequential lawlessness.
The one lost-in-jezebel pleads innocence and ignorance.
 The "I didn't know" and "I can't help it"
are deadly lies, meant to give you all the work of solving.

You can teach. You can witness.
 But you cannot choose for another.
 "Resist not" the evil choice.
  Leave it with God and let Him be God.

To the last moment of the final breath,
 there is hope for the person given to evil.

Until the judgment day of God's All Knowing,
He is ever extending mercy and kindness to
 His traitors.

The best bite of Christ's own dish,
 the "sop," was offered to Judas, minutes
  before the kiss of betrayal.

There is no greater test of fidelity than to give God-endued
freedom to the one who is the very worker of His Enemy
when it comes against... **you.**

Only Christ is capable of this. Only Christ **in you**
can "resist not the evil men do."
And only Christ in you will know when
to call down fire,
when to hide, and...
how to die.

Only Love Will Battle

For all the evil Satan is ever constructing,
   the Love of God is the only Victory... for the victim.
     Love is *power* over evil.

Love can break the walls of deliberate delusion.
Love can rescue the prisoner out of Jezebel.

Only Love prays.
Love is the one power to battle.
Love is the sole power to endure.
And love alone forgives...

   If you are the victim of Jezebel,
   if you are the brunt of an Ahab
     and you cannot flee, then
     there is one solution –
   forgiveness by the blood and the cross.

   To be free of Jezebel tyranny,
   the person involved must be forgiven
   by a deep and real release,
     an acceptance under God,
     and the absence of revenge.

   And only profound love can possibly forgive
     Jezebel and Ahab tyranny.

244

What is Love?
John, the expert of Love, by being
the Lover on Jesus' breast, defined Love.

"This is love, that we walk
according to His commandments."
2 John 6

Love is obedience to Christ. This alone is love and
rises from Love… for Him. Not loving humanity first
but ever LOVE for the Lord.

His Love has many faces.
Foreign ways.
Strange acts.
To call the Pharisees vipers was Love.
Love enough to bombard their evil even if
it meant they killed Him for it.

Jesus threw His life away the moment He named their evil.
From that moment they plotted His murder.
He knew exactly what He would lose in the confrontation –
His *life!*
Such is *the willingness of Love*.

He, who knows the need and the way to
capture the captured…
He will do it by the power of Love.
But Love – real Love – is something we know not.

Love is confrontation. Love is blank Truth.
Love is tender mercy for the merciless.
Love is agony of soul for the selfish.
Love is loving your murderer...
But Love is also ferocious objection to evil,
especially to religious evil that
ruins God's reputation of Infinite Good
by claiming His throne and voice.

Love is Christ alone and Christ alone is real Truth.
Unvarnished. God's Truth. Not human opinion.

Only Love prays all the way
to the end of evil.

The one caught in Jezebel is a lost sheep.
And the Love of Christ will ever search
for the lamb lost in the grip of a wolf.
(Matt. 18)

But it takes violence to topple Jezebel.
Love, reckless toward its self...
Love, pure and unafraid.
That Love, alone, can throw her
from the tower of Jezebel evil
and set her prisoners free!
(Isaiah 61:1)

Love forgives and *only* Love forgives.
Forgiveness is a **power**...
a great and miraculous power.
It wrecks evil and humiliates Satan.

246

To forgive is to transcend justice.
It is the victory of Holiness.
And by forgiving, I receive my own healing
of the serpent-stings.

*"Just as Moses lifted up the snake in the desert,
so the son of Man must be lifted up
that everyone who believes in him
may have eternal life."*
John 3:14

Jesus is the only solution for you,
and for those who have chosen evil.
Jesus alone can bear the daily assault of Jezebel.
Christ's resurrection power within,
endures and conquers - all for you in your spirit.
Christ is the victory.

Look away to Him and be led in triumph!

Always! All glory to Him who bore such evil
for our liberty as the children of God!

*"But thanks be to God, who always leads us in
His triumph in Christ, and manifests
through us the sweet aroma of
the knowledge of Him in every place."*
2 Cor. 2:14

The Great and Terrible Day

Where Jezebel is raging in unchecked evil,
   we consider the scene of Christ and the Pharisees.
      He confronted vehemently, then walked away.
        He left but **never** ran. He named the evil, described
         its root, and then ended the conversation.
            (Matt. 23)

Listen to the ferocious words of John the Baptist toward
    the "religious" who came out to be baptized.
He scorned them as a *"brood of vipers,"*
          (Luke 3:7)

Then there is Paul who called down blindness on the
    Jewish sorcerer who interfered with his witness
   to the proconsul in Cyprus.
          (Acts 13:11)

New Testament power surpasses Old Testament fervor.

The only hope for a Jezebel-infested person,
   is a blazing confrontation
      from one infused with the Spirit's fire and energy.
        One whose self-defending flesh has died.

   When God commands the severing of a relationship,
obey quickly in His courage. Get out and get away!

Often with a person in Jezebel-rebellion,
only separation of relationship
and/or church discipline is sufficient shock
to cause a breakthrough.

Should an individual or church be unwilling or incapable
of such confrontation, Jezebel will rule and ravage.
And those who are loyal to God will be
hounded into hiding, chased away,
and some will die before their time.

The lone believer and the corporate Church MUST rise to
the God-won position of authority.
On the bent knee of surrendered searching, *She* must
find the power and direction of Her Head, Jesus Christ,
to rise up whenever Jezebel invades.
To stand, to declare God's will;
and with the very zeal of the Lord,
defend His sheep and His purpose.

The church that is committed only to "nice" and
will not confront evil
by the biblical mandate for church discipline,
is a church that will
be defeated by *religious* evil –
never to count for the Son of God.

The Elijah-anointing of uncompromising holiness
and fearless obedience
must be welcomed in the church;
more than that, fervently prayed into our midst.

The Great and Terrible Day is the Second Coming of Christ,
a day we have not yet seen, but one
the entire world will inevitably witness.

"Behold, I will send you Elijah the prophet
before the great and terrible day of the Lord comes."

"And he shall turn and reconcile the hearts
of the [estranged] fathers to the [ungodly] children,
and the hearts of the [rebellious] children
to [the piety of] their fathers
[a reconciliation produced by repentance of the ungodly],
lest I come and smite the land
with a curse and a ban of utter destruction."
Malachi 4:6 Amplified Bible
Last verse of the Old Testament

Repentance is the only hope and solution to
those serving Jezebel
and those trapped in Ahab.

Repentance is a gift of the Spirit… a mercy and privilege.
The Holy Spirit broods over the darkness
of our soul and when we will even slightly turn
toward God, the Holy Spirit will bestow
the privilege of wrenching repentance.

It is seeing your self as God sees you,
and this Light throws you to the floor of your
soul, wailing in sorrow.
Repentance is not "I'm sorry, I'll do better."

Repentance is an invasion of the Spirit
    penetrating the motive of the heart, down
    into the very hidden chambers of the unconscious.

This repentance is the entrance to the Kingdom
    and the only one!
    And repentance is the only hope for
    those who give their souls to Jezebel tyranny
    and those who acquiesce as Ahab.

God's great mercy and suffering love sends
    a fiery Elijah into the jezebel-ahab madness.

The place of the prophet is always
    an uncompromising call to repentance.
Whether it is a harsh word of fire given to the hardened
    or the gentle nudge the humble will hear.

The *power of God through the authority of Go*d
rests on the Elijah-prophet and his anointing is that
    of correction by confrontation.
It is a most serious matter when the prophet comes.
    To fail to hear brings terrible consequences.

If repentance comes and is heeded, if the dirge is
    played and you will mourn,
        there is hope for liberty from evil.

But you cannot experience forgiveness without repentance.
And you cannot be changed without the cleansing
    power of God's forgiveness.
                        (I John 1:9)

If Elijah will be Elijah, Jezebel-Ahab both
    will perish out of the individuals who live in
        that satanic evil,
    or else they will be thrown out of the
        Fellowship of Believers.

Let us dare to remember and believe
    that final dire prediction of Malachi who
        is quoting neither prophet nor man,
        but the Lord of hosts Himself:
            "[Lest] I come and smite the land with
            a curse and a ban of utter destruction."

The "earth" hangs in Eternal Suspension,
    awaiting the shift in balance of
    spiritual crisis either to the victory of the elijah-anointing
        or to God's own curse of destruction.

God Himself sends Elijah for the purpose of healing
    males and fathers, for resolving family divisions
        arising from deadly sins of defiance.

Should the ungodly and the rebellious refuse His call
    for deep repentance; should the stubborn
    resist or silence the prophet, something worse than
        Elijah-confrontation will come.
            God Himself will scourge the earth
            before…

    The Great and Terrible Day of the Lord.

Also by Martha Kilpatrick

All and Only
In these pages are piercing insights into the very flavor
of God amidst the struggles of humanity as told through
the lives of Abraham, David, Esther, Joseph and others.

Adoration
The story of Mary of Bethany, friend of Jesus, sharer of
His secrets. She abides. . .uninhibited and limitless,
an eternal emblem of adoration of Jesus.

Shulamite Ministries Ezine
(Free Monthly Internet Magazine)
http://shulamite.com/e-zine.html

For tape lists and additional information
please write to:

Martha Kilpatrick
Shulamite Ministries
Post Office Box 10
Suches, GA 30572

Or Call
1-888-355-5373

Visit us at:
www.shulamite.com